WOODWORKER'S HAND TOOLS

AN ESSENTIAL GUIDE

RICK PETERS

STERLING PUBLISHING CO., INC.
New York

Production Staff

Design: Sandy Freeman
Cover Design: Karen Nelson
Photography: Christopher J. Vendetta
Cover Photo: Bill Milne

Illustrations: Triad Design Group, Ltd.
Copy Editor: Barbara McIntosh Webb
Page Layout: Sandy Freeman
Index: Nan Badgett

**Library of Congress
Cataloging-in-Publication Data Available**

Published by Sterling Publishing Company, Inc.
387 Park Avenue South, New York, N.Y. 10016
©2001 by Rick Peters
Distributed in Canada by Sterling Publishing
^c/o Canadian Manda Group
One Atlantic Avenue, Suite 105
Toronto, Ontario, Canada M6K 3E7
Distributed in Great Britain and Europe by
Cassell PLC, Wellington House, 125 Strand,
London WC2R 0BB, England
Distributed in Australia by Capricorn Link
(Australia) Pty. Ltd.
P.O. Box 704, Windsor, NSW 2756 Australia

Printed in China
All rights reserved

Sterling ISBN 0-8069-6661-0

CONTENTS

ACKNOWLEDGMENTS

For all their help, advice, and support, I offer special thanks to:

Christopher Vendetta, ace photographer, for taking such beautiful photographs in less than desirable conditions (my dusty workshop) and under such tight deadlines.

William Warner, antique tool aficionado, for allowing Chris and me to come into his home and photograph just a tiny portion of his incredible tool collection. All of the luscious tools shown in the beginning of each chapter are from William's collection.

David Sendall with American Tool Companies, Inc., manufacturers of such trusted names as Marples, Record, Irwin, and Quick-Grip, for supplying numerous products, photos, illustrations, and technical information.

John Economaki of Bridge City Tool Works for lending me just a small portion of the fabulous measurement and layout tools they manufacture.

Tom Lie-Nielsen of Lie-Nielsen Toolworks, Inc., for supplying me with some of his world-class planes, saws, and scrapers. (Sure, I'm sending them back, Tom. They're in the mail—really.)

Jessica Burtt with DMT (Diamond Machining Technology, Inc.) for supplying photos, product, and technical information on their most excellent diamond stones.

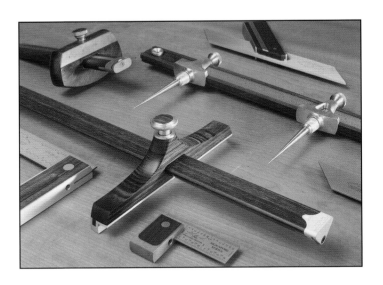

Sandy Freeman, book designer extraordinaire, whose exquisite art talents are evident on every page of this book.

Barb Webb, copyediting whiz, for ferreting out mistakes and gently suggesting corrections.

Greg Kopfer with the Triad Design Group for his superb illustrations.

Heartfelt thanks to my family: Cheryl, Lynne, Will, and Beth, for putting up with the craziness that goes with writing a book and living with a woodworker: late nights, short weekends, wood everywhere, noise from the shop, and sawdust footprints in the house.

And finally, words can't express my gratitude to my wife, Cheryl, for taking off the rough edges and smoothing out the manuscript. Thanks, Love.

INTRODUCTION

My love of hand tools began when my mom gave me a tool set for my sixth birthday. You may even know it—the classic Popular Mechanics blue-handled tools in the wood case. Man, I loved that set. Even though it was almost bigger than me, I'd tote it around the house "fixing" things. One of the first things I "fixed" was a coffee table in the front room that was too high for me. Out came the ruler to carefully measure 6" up from the bottom of each leg. Then I used my very own saw to lop off each leg at the mark: a lot of work, but I was the "man" for the job. Heck, I even sanded the bottom of each leg before flipping the table back over (no simple task when you're six).

Mom, needless to say, was not impressed. The saw went away. And over the next few weeks, so did almost everything else, one tool at a time, until I was left with a ruler and a try square (do you know how much neat stuff is inside a toaster?). Anyway, my passion for tools was so strong and so obvious that I often received tools instead of toys as gifts at Christmas or birthdays. My brother Jim gave me my first real toolbox: a blue metal union-made box. I still have it. At ages 10 and 11, I received my first power tools, a Black & Decker jigsaw and finish sander (now collectors' items; still have them, too).

Although now I have a fully equipped shop that rivals Norm's, I still love my hand tools and I use them every chance I get. Occasionally, I'll build something completely by hand just to slow things down and "connect" with the wood. Working wood with hand tools for me has always been a joyful experience that I just don't get from power tools. It's very personal—the feel of the wood as it responds to the tool's edge. There's nothing quite like it.

If you haven't had the chance to build something entirely by hand, especially if you start with a rough-sawn plank and hand-plane it, I heartily recommend it. Even if it looks awful in the end (like my first dovetailed box—yikes!), you'll be glad you made the effort. If nothing else, it will give you a profound appreciation for cabinetmakers of yore. You might even get hooked.

Just stay away from the coffee table.

Rick Peters
Fall 2001

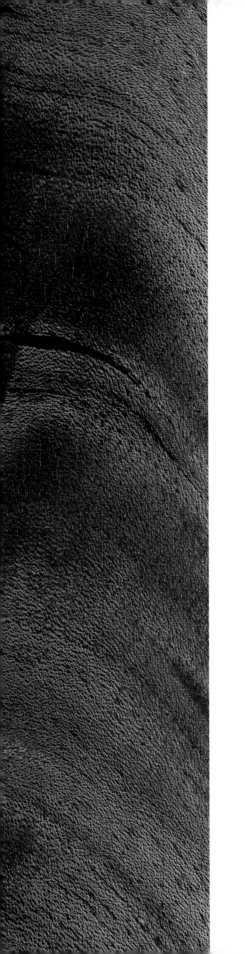

"...for the strength and durability of any structure, independent of the material, depends on precision, and any inaccuracy not only frequently impairs outward beauty, but produces, in a corresponding degree, a real want of firmness and stability."

BLACKIE & SONS (1853)

MEASURING and MARKING TOOLS

In woodworking, doing a project "by the numbers" isn't a mark of mediocrity, or same old same old; it's absolutely vital. The "numbers" involved, of course, are the dimensions of the wood being worked. When you don't measure and lay out with precision—as Mr. Blackie notes—you can end up with a piece that lacks not only beauty but also durability.

Your shop tools might be the finest and sharpest available. But if you can't both measure and mark accurately, those tools are virtually worthless.

Look at the rosewood, ivory, and brass in the photo at left—this wasn't mere indulgence. Woodworkers of yore knew that these quality materials were worth the relative high cost at the time (just one of these beauties could have cost a couple of months' worth of wages). Our predecessors in the craft understood the importance of buying quality to create quality. And like famed cabinetmakers Blackie & Sons, they knew full well the importance of precision. There are lots of steps involved in crafting a fine piece with confidence—and every one relies on going "by the numbers."

Clockwise from top left: an "American Combined Level and Grade Finder," patented in 1904; a handmade 24" panel gauge; a folding rule No. 15, made by C. S. Co.; calipers (brass with steel legs); Stanley No. 5 trammel points; a 7 1/2" combined try and miter square, made by Stanley Tools; a Stanley No. 7 scratch awl; Henry Disston and Sons' mortise gauge; and a Stanley No. 40 ivory and German silver caliper rule.

Marking Tools

If you were to ask most woodworkers what the foundation of accuracy is, they'd likely say the ruler, the tape measure, or the square. But I've always felt it's the marking tools you choose. Granted, the rule, tape measure, and square are essential to precision; but without a clean, crisp marking tool, all their accuracy is for naught.

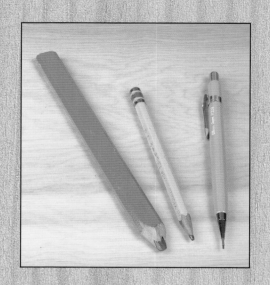

Pencils

The most common marking tool in the shop is a pencil (*top photo*). A carpenter's pencil is not suitable for intricate layout work; with its thick lead and cumbersome body, it's best left for initial layout of rough boards. Many woodworkers use a standard No. 2 pencil for their layout work. This is certainly better than a carpenter's pencil, but it can still add significant errors to your work. The reason is that the line thickness varies as the lead wears (*middle drawing*). This might seem trivial, but it's not.

Say, for example, you're laying out dovetails for a set of drawers. If you use a standard pencil, the lead will wear considerably. Unless you constantly sharpen it, you can introduce anywhere from $1/32$" to $1/16$" of error from start to finish (no wonder those dovetails don't fit!). My choice for all-around layout work is a mechanical pencil with a 5mm lead. This leaves a crisp, even line—even as it wears.

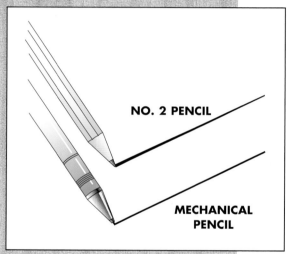

NO. 2 PENCIL

MECHANICAL PENCIL

Marking knives

When accuracy is paramount, I reach for a marking knife (*bottom photo*). As long as it's sharp, a marking knife produces an extremely fine line on a board. On the plus side, this can help guide a chisel or saw during a cut. The downside to this is that cutting into the wood can leave marks that may need to be removed later.

In addition to pencils and marking knives, there are three other marking tools I like to have on hand in the shop: a lumber crayon, white marking pencils, and a chalk line.

Lumber crayons

A lumber crayon is designed to mark on rough-cut lumber (*top photo*). Though you can use a pencil for this, a lumber crayon will serve you better, especially if the wood isn't completely dry. Pencil marks tend to absorb into the surface of the wood over time and disappear. A lumber crayon's marks are impervious to this. As a matter of fact, most sawmills mark freshly cut wood with a lumber crayon before it goes into the kiln for drying; after the wood comes out, the crayon's marks are still legible.

White pencils

Another nifty marking tool to have on hand is a white pencil for drawing on dark woods, where a pencil line would blend into the wood and be invisible (*middle photo*). White pencils can be found at most art centers as either a standard colored pencil, a grease pencil, or a marker. All of these work well, but I prefer a white colored pencil—just make sure to sharpen it frequently if accuracy is an issue.

Chalk lines

Chalk lines are useful for marking long, straight lines, such as when preparing rough stock or sizing long boards (*bottom photo*). Make sure to shake the chalk line before use to evenly coat the line, and then hook the end over the board at your mark. Stretch the line to the opposite end of the board and pull the line straight up a couple of inches; then let go to "snap" a line on the board.

AWLS

The awl has historically been used to create starter holes in wood for brads and nails, and to create starting points for drill bits. The most common type of awl is the scratch awl (*top photo*). As you can see, the size and length of the awl can vary greatly, but each has a cylindrical shaft that tapers to a point. Another type of awl (not shown here) that's very hard to find anymore is a brad awl. The tip of this awl comes to a chisel point, much like screwdriver. A brad awl was used in the past to create starter holes in tougher hardwoods, where the grain would often deflect a scratch awl. The chisel point of the brad awl was aligned with the grain at the mark, then pushed in and twisted to cut a small hole. These have been superseded by the centerpunch (*page* 12).

Marking hole locations

In my shop, I frequently use an awl as a centerpunch to mark hole locations. An awl is especially useful when marking holes using a template (*middle photo*). That's because the thin tapered shank can pass through the holes in a template, where the blunt tip of a centerpunch can't get through.

Basic grip

To use an awl as a centerpunch or to create starter holes for nails or brads, nestle the handle of the awl in the palm of your hand as shown in the bottom photo, and then wrap your fingers around the handle. This grip positions the awl in line with your forearm so you'll transfer maximum thrust into the workpiece.

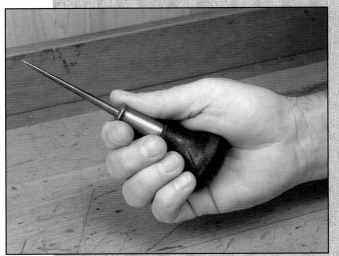

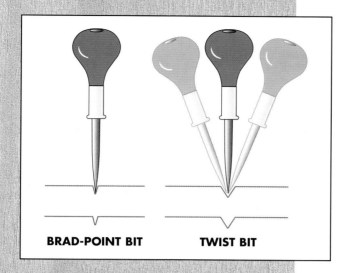

BRAD-POINT BIT   **TWIST BIT**

Wobble if necessary

If you do use an awl in place of a centerpunch, you may or may not want to wobble the awl—it all depends on the drill bit you're using. If it's a brad-point bit, or a Forstner bit, a single thrust into the wood will do. However, when using a twist bit, I've found that if I enlarge the hole by wobbling the awl (*top drawing*), the tip of the bit will have less tendency to wander.

As a holder

But an awl can be used for much more than marking starter holes. It's also useful as a holder or a "third hand," and as a marking tool. I often use an awl as an all-purpose holder to temporarily fasten thin materials together, or as the pivot point when scribing a long, graceful arc with a thin strip of wood and a pencil (*middle photo*). An awl is equally effective as a "third hand" when you're working by yourself with long boards or with anything greater than your arm span: Just secure the end of a tape measure or chalk line to a workpiece with an awl, and then stretch it to the opposite end to measure or snap a line.

Marking

I've known quite a few woodworkers who prefer a sharp awl to a pencil. The thin, tapered blades of awls make them particularly useful for reaching into tight quarters, such as when marking pins for dovetails. You can use one in lieu of a marking knife (*bottom photo*); just make sure to keep the point razor-sharp, as it will tend to tear wood fibers instead of cutting them like a knife.

CENTERPUNCHES

Although a centerpunch is often thought of as a machinist's tool, many woodworkers (including myself) find them useful in the shop. When I have a lot of holes to mark for drilling, I usually reach for a centerpunch or for my automatic centerpunch (*top photo*). Also, since I often incorporate metal into the jigs, fixtures, and projects I build, a centerpunch is the best tool for marking hole locations. You'd quickly dull the point on a standard scratch awl if you were to use it, instead of a centerpunch, on metal.

Automatic centerpunch

An automatic centerpunch has an internal spring that releases when the tool is depressed, forcing an internal plunger or anvil to strike the tip and leave a dimple on the workpiece (*middle drawing*). The springs on most automatic centerpunches are adjustable so that you can vary the depth of the dimple.

Tip angle

Depending on what material you're drilling into, you may want to have a couple of centerpunches, each with the tip ground to a different angle (*bottom drawing*). If you're drilling into metal with twist bits, you'll want an angle somewhere around 60 degrees to match the angle of the twist bit. For marking in wood where you'll be drilling with a brad-point or Forstner bit, you'll find that an angle around 45 degrees works best. ShopTip: If accuracy is critical when locating a hole in wood, your best bet is to make a small dimple in the wood with an awl, and then use this as a starting point for a centerpunch.

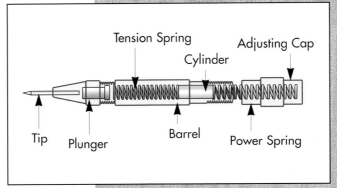

Tension Spring

Cylinder

Adjusting Cap

Tip

Plunger

Barrel

Power Spring

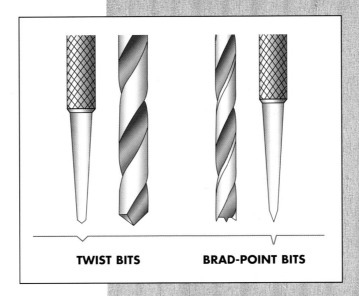

TWIST BITS   **BRAD-POINT BITS**

RULES

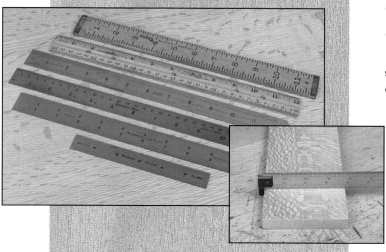

If you told me I could have only one measuring tool in the shop, I'd be hard-pressed to decide between the 6" metal rule that lives in one apron pocket and the 12-foot Starrett tape measure in the other. Although you might think I'd go for the tape measure, I'd stick with the metal rule. Why? It's more accurate, not only for laying out joints, but also for checking them: A tape measure just doesn't slip into a tongue or rabbet cut in the edge of a board like a metal rule does. Fortunately, I don't have to make that call.

Type of rules

Woodworkers can choose from a wide variety of rules made of either metal or wood (*top photo*). I much prefer a metal rule because its thinness reduces problems with parallax associated with the thicker wooden rules. In my shop I have a 6", 12", 18", and 1-meter metal rule. Another specialty rule is a hook rule (*top inset*). It has a plastic hook on one end that catches the edge of the workpiece for super-accurate measuring. When buying a rule, check to make sure that the graduations are etched into the metal and not simply printed on (*middle photo*). Printed graduations can wear off over time.

CHECKING A RULE

For a rule to have any worth, it must be accurate. Check the graduations of your rules against each other—you may be surprised to find that they're not the same. The two rules in the photo at near right are off almost ¹/₃₂". This is an excellent reason to use a single rule throughout a project; if you use multiple rules and tape measures, you may inject errors that cannot be traced. Also, check your rules for flatness (*photo below right*). Set a rule on a known-flat surface and place a pair of flat scraps (called winding sticks) on the rule. Sight along the tops of the sticks to check for twist; replace any rules that aren't absolutely flat.

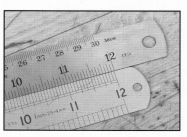

LAYOUT TIPS

Block of wood

A common cause of inaccuracy when using a metal rule is in measuring in from the edge of a workpiece. The problem is positioning the rule so that it's absolutely flush with the edge. Many woodworkers use their finger as a stop and press the rule into their finger. Good idea, but the rule will often go past the edge when pressed into the resilient flesh. A better solution is to use a scrap of wood as a stop (*top photo*). I always have a few small scraps of MDF (medium-density fiberboard) lying around just for this. MDF is super-flat and resistant to warp. Just press the scrap firmly against the edge of the workpiece and then butt the end of the rule up against the scrap.

Center of a board

Here's a quick tip for finding the center of a board with a rule. Position one end of the rule flush with the edge of the workpiece (the scrap block tip mentioned above works great here). Then pivot the rule until a number that's easily divisible by 2 rests directly over the opposite edge. Divide this number in half and mark the center (*middle drawing*).

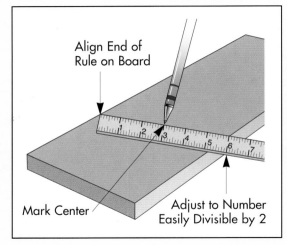

Align End of Rule on Board

Mark Center

Adjust to Number Easily Divisible by 2

Dividing a board equally

Quick: You need to divide a board that's 9 ⅝" wide into five equal parts. The solution? Modify the "center of a board" trick above. Place an end of the rule flush with one edge of the workpiece. Pivot the rule until a number (10, in this case) that's easily divisible by the desired units rests directly over the opposite edge. Then mark to create equal spacing (*bottom drawing*).

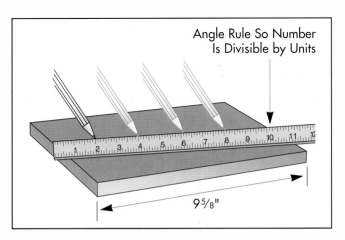

Angle Rule So Number Is Divisible by Units

9 ⅝"

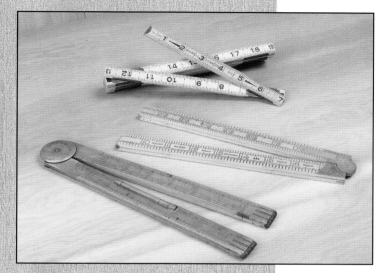

FOLDING RULES

Long before the tape measure arrived, the folding rule was used for layout and measuring (*top photo*). Typically made of boxwood with brass protecting the ends, the most common of these was the four-fold 2-foot rule that fit easily in a pocket. A more modern type of folding rule is the zigzag rule (*background in top photo*). Although I usually use a tape measure in the shop, I often reach for a folding or zigzag rule when measuring inside dimensions, or anytime that the flexibility of a tape would cause a measurement error.

Extension

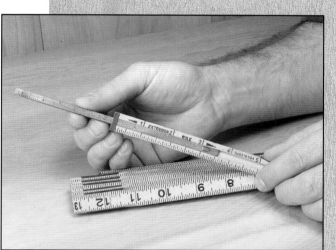

One advantage some zigzag rules have over a folding rule is that they often have a built-in extension (*middle photo*). This extension is a metal bar that slides out of one end to make inside measurements a snap. (See page 17 for a tip on making accurate inside measurements with a tape measure.)

LEVEL AND PROTRACTOR

Folding rules were in use for many years before the tape measure took over, and they evolved to offer extra bells and whistles that today's tape measures don't. Shown in the photo *above right* are two features that were quite common: a built-in level and a set of marks on the pivot point for accurately

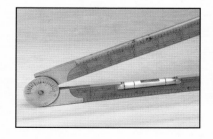

setting angles. Here's a good example of an older tool that can do more than its modern equivalent. This theme recurs throughout this book because I'm a fan of old tools—not just because they're old, but because they're often made better than today's tools and offer features you just can't find anymore.

TAPE MEASURES

I'm sure that when Alvin J. Fellows patented the steel tape measure in 1868, he didn't expect that his invention would turn out to be one of the most useful of all tools to the woodworker. Although his tape measure didn't have a locking mechanism for the tape (this was patented by Stanley in 1968), his was the first to print accurate graduations on a steel tape. Today's tape measures feature spring-loaded tapes that are slightly concave to help hold them rigid over long distances. They're commonly available in 8-, 12-, 16-, and 25-foot lengths. I've always found the combination of a smaller 12-foot and a larger 25-foot tape measure to be all that I need in the shop (*top photo*).

Checking a tape

When you're buying a tape measure, skip the bargain bin; it pays to buy quality. Go with a name brand you can trust, like Starrett, Stanley, or Lufkin. And, take the time to check it for accuracy at the store. To do this, simply extend the tape out several feet and bend it back on itself. Align the inch marks and check to see whether the graduations are even (*middle photo*). On cheaper tapes, you'll often find that the graduations don't match up.

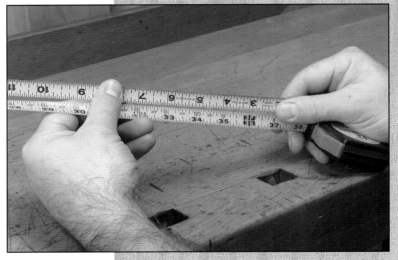

The hook

Another thing to check for when buying a tape measure is a quality hook that's securely riveted to the end of the tape, while still allowing it to move freely for inside and outside measurements. The reason the hook needs to slide is for inside measurements: It's designed to slide in the exact thickness of the hook to provide an accurate measurement (*bottom drawing*).

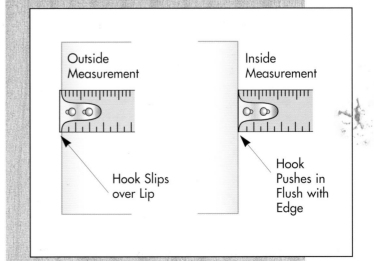

Outside Measurement

Inside Measurement

Hook Slips over Lip

Hook Pushes in Flush with Edge

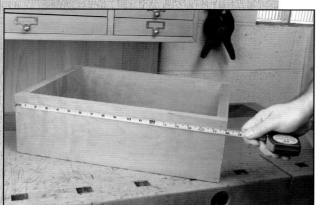

Inside measurements

Most quality tape measures will have the exact dimensions of the case printed directly on the side of the case. This makes it easy to take an inside measurement. Just butt the case of the tape measure firmly against the side of the workpiece and extend the tape to the other side (*top photo*). With this in mind, you're always better off choosing a tape measure whose outside case dimensions are easy to work with—it's a lot simpler to add 3" to $9^{7}/_{16}$" than $2^{1}/_{2}$". Try to find a case with an even inch dimension.

Outside measurements

An outside measurement is simplicity itself: Just catch the edge of the hook on one edge of the workpiece, and pull to extend the tape (*middle photo*). You're always better off pivoting the tape so that it lies flat on the edge to be measured. This positions the tape flush with the surface and prevents errors from parallax.

ACCURACY TIPS

The methods described above work fine for general-purpose inside and outside measurements. But when you're looking for added precision, try these two tricks:

1. For inside measurements, butt a reference block up against an inside edge of the workpiece (I have a scrap of MDF cut precisely to 4" set aside just for instances like this). Then extend the tape to the opposite end and read where it passes over the reference block—add the length of the block to this to get a super-accurate reading (*top photo at right*).

2. For outside measurements, try extending the hook end of the tape 1" past the edge of the workpiece (*bottom photo at right*). Take the reading and subtract an inch. This method eliminates any error caused by a bent or malfunctioning hook.

TRY SQUARES

Try squares have long been a mainstay of the woodworker. We use them to lay out and mark boards for joinery, and to check edges to make sure they're truly square. A try square consists of a metal blade and either a wood or metal stock (*top photo*). Most quality wood stocks have the edges faced with brass to reduce wear. Although an engineer's square (*see page* 19) does the same job as a try square, with a higher degree of accuracy, I still like the feel of a wood-handled try square; but when accuracy is critical, I'll reach for an engineer's square.

A specialized version of the try square is the miter square (*inset*). It serves the same function as a try square, but the blade is inset in the stock at 45 degrees for checking and laying out miters.

Photo courtesy of Bridge City Tool Works, copyright 2001

Checking a try square

Just like any other layout tool, if a try square isn't accurate, it's not worth much. To see whether a try square is actually square, place the stock up against a known-flat edge (*middle drawing*). Then draw a line along the blade and flip the stock over. Align the blade with the line you just drew—it should be in perfect alignment. If not, you'll have to adjust either the stock or the blade by filing it down. (For a nifty alternative to this, see the sidebar below.)

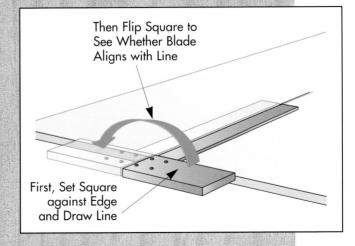

Then Flip Square to See Whether Blade Aligns with Line

First, Set Square against Edge and Draw Line

ADJUSTABLE SQUARES

Even though I prefer a try square with a wood stock, these can go out of square over time. That's because the wood in the stock is constantly moving to react to changes in relative humidity. This can loosen the rivets that hold the blade in place, allowing it to shift out of square. Bridge City Tool Works produces a set of adjustable squares designed to get around this problem. You can tweak the angle of the blade with an Allen wrench (*photo at left*).

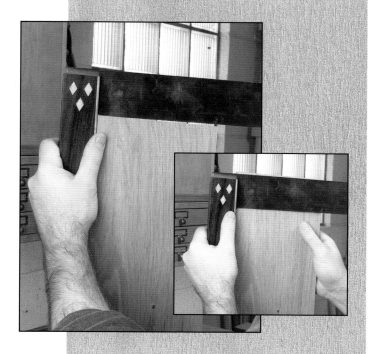

Checking an edge for square

The most accurate way to use a try square when checking for square is to position the blade of the square against the edge of the workpiece (*top photo*). This lets you position the workpiece so that light can shine through from behind to indicate any gaps. The less desirable method is to place the blade on the face of the workpiece and slide it up until it's near the end of the workpiece (*inset*). It's difficult to see any gaps this way; avoid it whenever possible.

Accurate marking

If you've ever watched a draftsman in action, you'll note that he always places his pencil at the exact point where he wants to draw a line, and slides the square up so it butts up against the pencil (*middle drawing*). This might seem like a no-brainer, but over the years I've watched a lot of woodworkers do just the opposite—set the square on the mark and then draw the line. The problem with this is that it doesn't take into account the distance between the square and the centerpoint of the pencil lead.

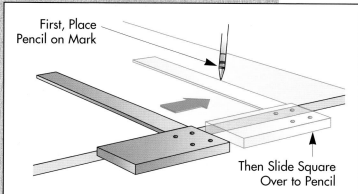

First, Place Pencil on Mark

Then Slide Square Over to Pencil

ENGINEER'S SQUARES

Engineer's squares are similar to try squares except both the stock and the blade are metal, and they're manufactured to much higher tolerances. I use them whenever accuracy is critical, and I've found the small size indispensable for checking for square. As a matter of fact, the small one shown here is a constant companion to the tape measure and 6" metal rule that reside in my apron pockets.

LEVELS

While many woodworkers think of a level as a carpenter's tool, it has a place in every shop. A level, particularly a torpedo level, is handy for checking that shelves are level, cabinets are hung plumb, and workbenches and tools are level (*top photo*).

Types of levels

The most common levels are 3 or 4 feet in length, with bodies made of wood, metal, or plastic. Virtually every level has multiple vials, which are curved glass or plastic tubes filled with alcohol (hence the name "spirit" level). A bubble of air trapped in the vial will always float to the highest point on the curve. Marks on each side of the centerpoint indicate level or plumb. While steel I-beam–style levels (*center level in middle photo*) are accurate and lightweight, I still prefer the warmth of the older wood-and-brass levels of yesteryear (*top level in middle photo*).

Checking a level

Can a level go out of whack? You bet. Here's how to check to make sure your level is on the level. Place the level on a known-flat surface and mark its exact location with a pencil (*bottom drawing*). Note the bubble reading on the vials with a pencil mark as well, and then flip the level end for end, aligning it with the pencil marks. Check the bubbles and then repeat by flipping the level upside down. All of the bubble readings should match. If they don't, most levels have adjustable vials to make this correction. Loosen the screws, adjust the vial positions, and repeat until all readings are the same.

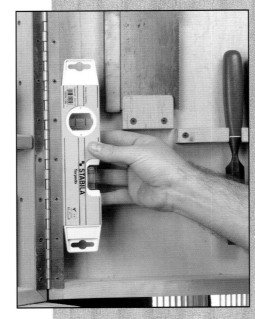

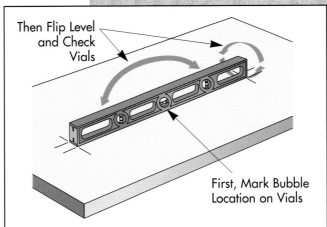

Then Flip Level and Check Vials

First, Mark Bubble Location on Vials

COMBINATION SQUARES

What do you get when you combine a metal rule, try square, miter square, level, and depth gauge into one tool? A combination square (*top photo*). A combination square is a metal rule with a groove in it that accepts a pin in the head of the square. The head has two faces—one at 90 degrees and the other at 45 degrees. When the knurled nut on the end of the pin is tightened, the head locks the rule in place at the desired location. Some heads also incorporate a spirit level, but the short length of the head (typically 4") limits its usefulness. While most combination squares come with only one head, there are two other accessory heads that are quite useful: a center-finding head and a protractor head that adjusts to any angle from 0 to 180 degrees (*inset*).

As a try square

Probably the most ordinary use of a combination square is as a try square (*middle photo*). The advantage to using a combination square is that you can adjust the blade to the desired length. Also, since its head is metal, a combination square is usually more accurate than a try square with a wood stock.

As a depth gauge

Another frequent use of a combination square is as a depth gauge (*bottom photo*). To use one for this purpose, loosen its knurled knob and place the 90-degree face of the head so that it spans the hole to be measured. Make sure all chips are cleared from the hole, and then lower the blade until it bottoms out. Tighten the knurled knob and remove the blade to read the depth.

Parallel lines

By far the most common reason I reach for a combination square is that I need to mark out a line parallel to an edge or a series of parallel lines. The combination square really excels here. Say, for instance, you want to lay out a series of lines on a fireplace mantel where you're going to carve a set of flutes. Just set the blade the desired distance from the edge of the work-piece, lock it in place, and then butt the head up against the edge of the workpiece (*top photo*). You'll note that there's a small notch centered in the end of the metal rule; this is for your pencil (or awl, if you prefer). Position the pencil in the notch, and while holding it firmly in place, slide the square along the edge of the workpiece, keeping steady pressure on the head.

PARALLEL LINES WITHOUT A COMBINATION SQUARE

If you don't have a combination square and need to lay out parallel lines, here are a couple of ways to do it. I had an old-timer woodworker friend who could mark out parallel lines with just a pencil with unbelievable accuracy. He'd hold the pencil in his hand and use his fingers as a stop to position the pencil where he needed it (*top photo at right*). He'd been doing this for so long, he could hit a mark within about $1/32$". Although I'm not that accurate, I often use this method when I'm marking out a detail that doesn't require absolute precision, like the chamfer around the edge of a table top.

If you've got a lot of parallel lines to draw that need to be precise, consider constructing a simple shop-made square (*bottom photo*). It's just a block of wood that's notched the desired distance in from the edge. A kerf in the end of the scrap accepts a pencil to draw uniformly accurate lines.

CENTER-FINDING TIPS

You'll frequently need to find the center of a workpiece. The combination square is the perfect tool for the job. Here are three different ways to use it to locate dead center.

Marking diagonals

The first and simplest method to locate center is to use the 45-degree head of the square to mark a series of diagonals (*top photo*). This method works best with stock that is relatively square, since sides that are not 90-degree can throw the centerpoint off.

Using a center-finding head

If you've purchased the center-finding head for your combination square, it doesn't get any easier than this. Just slip the center-finding head on the blade and position the head so it touches adjacent sides of the workpiece; then mark center (*middle photo*). This head is especially useful for finding center on round stock.

With a framing square

The only disadvantage to the methods described above is that they work well only for relatively small workpieces. If you have a workpiece that's larger than 6" to 7", you might find that this tip works well:

Clamp a framing square to the blade of the combination square so that the long blade butts up against the 45-degree face of the combination square's head (*bottom photo*). Adjust the blade of the combination square so that it bisects the inside corner of the framing square. Then position the framing square so that both its legs contact the workpiece, and mark the center.

FRAMING SQUARES

A framing square is another one of the tools that some woodworkers feel belong only in a carpenter's toolbox. That's too bad, because a framing square is quite useful in the woodshop. The longer legs of a framing square make it ideal for checking larger surfaces, where a smaller try square or combination square won't give an accurate reading. Framing squares can be found in a number of materials and sizes (*top photo*). I prefer an aluminum square over a steel one, as it's much lighter and won't rust over time.

Checking a framing square

To make sure your framing square is accurate, place it on a workpiece with a known straight front edge. Position the square so the short leg (the tongue) extends just over the edge of the workpiece. Then draw a line along the long leg (the blade) and flip the square over (*middle drawing*). Slide the square over until the blade aligns with the line you've just drawn—it should line up perfectly. If it doesn't, you can retrue the square by lightly hammering the metal at the diagonal joint between the tongue and the blade. If you hammer on the inside edge, the square will "open"; hammering on the outside corner "closes" the square.

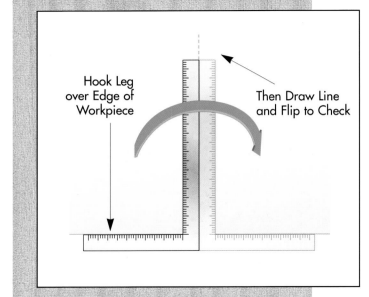

Hook Leg over Edge of Workpiece

Then Draw Line and Flip to Check

Accuracy tip

Whenever you're looking for added accuracy with a framing square, allow the tongue or blade of the square to hang down over the edge of the workpiece and press it firmly against the edge (*bottom photo*). This ensures that the square will be aligned perfectly with the edge. It's easy to introduce error here if you simply try to hold the tongue flush with the edge with the square on top of the workpiece.

MARKING GAUGES

Marking gauges are extremely useful for marking lines parallel to an edge with great accuracy, such as when you're laying out joints to be cut. A marking gauge basically consists of four parts: a beam, a fence (or stock), a thumbscrew, and a marking pin. The beam and fence may be made of wood or metal. Wood marking gauges are more common and may or may not have brass strips inlaid to reduce wear (*top photo*). Some beams have scales, but these are best used only to set the fence to an approximate distance.

Basic use

To use a marking gauge, loosen the thumbscrew and slide the fence the desired distance from the pin. Tighten the thumbscrew and make a test mark; readjust as necessary. Place the fence of the gauge up against the edge of the workpiece and angle it so the pin tilts away from the direction you'll move the square (*middle photo*). Although most woodworkers feel they have better control pushing the gauge, there's no reason not to pull it if this feels better to you.

Steady, even pressure

A marking gauge will accurately scribe parallel lines as long as you use steady, even pressure to hold the fence firmly against the edge of the workpiece (*bottom drawing*). If you don't, the pin can and will wander. Pressing firmly will also keep the beam parallel to the surface, which will prevent the pin from scribing at an angle.

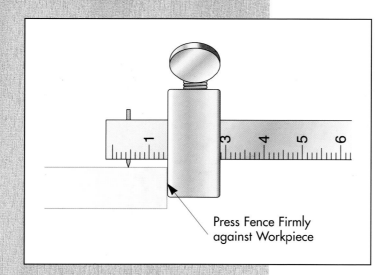

Press Fence Firmly against Workpiece

CUTTING GAUGE

A cutting gauge is very similar to a marking gauge except that instead of using a pin to mark the workpiece, it uses a knife (*top photo*). The advantage to this is that the knife cleanly cuts through the wood fibers instead of tearing them, as a pin does. This makes a cutting gauge the tool of choice whenever you need to mark lines across grain.

You might then think, why not throw out my marking gauge and just use the cutting gauge? Because since the knife of a cutting gauge leaves such a thin, crisp line, it virtually disappears when you use it to scribe a line along the grain. ShopTip: To create a "universal" marking gauge, some woodworkers file the point of their marking gauge to a finer point. This does an adequate job of marking both with and against the grain, but is still inferior to results from the individual gauges.

Basic use

The technique for using a cutting gauge is virtually identical to that of the marking gauge, with one exception: Take care to use very light pressure (*middle photo*). If the knife is sharp (a few licks with a diamond hone will bring it to a crisp point), it's easy to cut deeply into the wood, leaving cross-grain scratches that can be a hassle to remove.

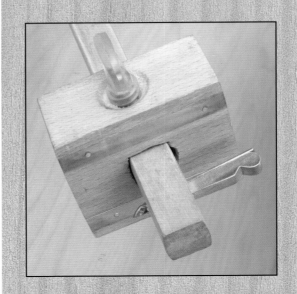

VENEER STRIP TIP

A cutting gauge can also be pressed into service to create uniform strips of veneer to use as inlay for your projects (*photo at left*). Set the fence to the desired strip width, and place the veneer on a scrap piece so it's flush with the edge. Make a series of light cuts to produce strips.

MORTISE GAUGES

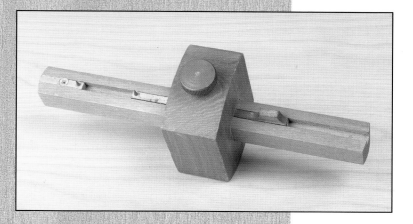

A mortise gauge has two pins instead of one to simultaneously mark out two parallel lines. It's designed specifically to lay out the cheeks of mortises and tenons. One of the pins is fixed, while the other is independently adjustable (*top photo*). In some cases, this pin adjusts via a simple pull slide; on others there's a thumbscrew or knurled knob mounted to the end of the beam. Many mortise gauges also feature a third pin on the beam opposite the two mortise pins. This allows the mortise gauge to also function as a marking gauge.

Setting the pins

The first step in using a mortise gauge is to set the pins. To do this, hold the mortise chisel up to the pins, adjust the traveling pin over to match the width of the chisel, and lock it in place (*middle photo*). Then slide the fence over so the pins are set the desired distance from the edge of the workpiece. Try the setup on a scrap piece first, and check the layout with a rule. Readjust as necessary.

Basic use

Just as with the marking gauge or the cutting gauge, the critical thing here is to firmly press the stock up against the edge of the workpiece. All you're looking for here is steady, even pressure. Popeye-like strength will only cause problems—most commonly, excess pressure will shift the position of the traveling pin or the beam. Use a light, firm grip, and tilt the gauge away from the direction of movement (*bottom photo*).

PANEL GAUGES

A panel gauge is basically a wood marking gauge that's designed to handle big panels. The difference is the beam is much longer (typically 15" to 30") than a standard gauge and the fence is much wider. In the past, panel gauges were often made of mahogany with brass wear fittings. The exquisite one shown here (*top photo*) is made by Bridge City Tool Works (www.bridgecitytools.com) and will mark to the center of a 48"-wide workpiece. You can also regularly find antique panel gauges on the Internet at various sites, running anywhere from $20 to $40 for a gauge in good condition.

Photo courtesy of Bridge City Tool Works, copyright 2001

Two hands

Using a panel gauge is definitely a two-handed operation. After you've loosened the thumbscrew (older versions often use a wedge to lock the beam in position) and adjusted the pin or knife the desired distance from the edge, lock the beam in place. Then press the fence firmly against the edge of the workpiece with one hand while you apply light downward pressure to the pin or knife with your other hand (*middle photo*). Move the gauge slowly with steady, even pressure.

Cutting disc

Instead of a pin or knife, the Bridge City panel gauge shown here uses a cutting disc (*bottom photo*). The disc is made of hardened steel and is beveled to help pull the fence into the workpiece as you move the gauge along the edge of the workpiece. This leaves razor-sharp lines with no tear-out, even when you're cutting across the grain.

DOVETAIL GAUGES

A dovetail gauge (or dovetail marker) is a single-use tool that's designed to lay out the pins and tails for dovetail joints. Quality dovetail gauges will offer the two most common angles for dovetails: a 1:8 slope for hardwoods and a 1:6 slope for softwoods. If you generally use these two slopes, a dovetail gauge or set of markers like those shown in the top photo will serve you well (the gold marker is for hardwoods, the dark marker for softwoods). If you prefer to set your own angles, a bevel gauge (*page* 30) is a better choice.

Tails

To use a dovetail marker, first use a marking or cutting gauge to set the depth of the tails to match the thickness of the wood. Then carefully lay out the tail spacing. Position the dovetail marker so it aligns with one of the marks and so the slope is in the correct direction. Then use a pencil or marking knife to mark the side of the tail (*middle photo*). Flip the marker over and mark the opposite side. Continue like this until all the tails have been marked.

Pins

Depending on how you cut your dovetails (I always cut the tails first and then use them to locate the pins), you may or may not want to mark the pins at the same time you lay out the tails. Whichever method you choose, align the marker with the layout marks that you made on the end of the workpiece and mark their location with a pencil or marking knife (*bottom photo*).

BEVEL GAUGES

A bevel gauge (or sliding T-bevel) is an invaluable layout tool in the shop. You can use it to verify angles, set tools to match angles, and lay out virtually any angle. Most bevel gauges feature a metal slotted blade and a stock or body made of wood, plastic, or metal, available in a variety of sizes (*top photo*). The blade conveniently slips into the slot in the body for storage. The blade is locked in place by tightening a thumbscrew, wing nut, lever, or knob at the base of the stock.

Duplicating an angle

A common use of the bevel gauge is to duplicate an angle so that you can reproduce it. To do this, loosen the thumbscrew or wing nut so it's friction-tight, and press the stock of the gauge up against the edge of the workpiece (*middle photo*). Then angle the blade until it rests on the angled end of the workpiece. Tighten the wing nut, and then use the gauge to duplicate this angle on another workpiece.

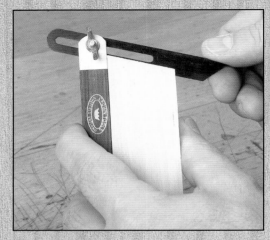

Setting with a protractor

In many cases you'll want to set the bevel gauge to an exact angle, or read the angle you've just set (such as when you're duplicating an angle). The most accurate way to do this is to use a protractor. The critical point here is to make sure that the blade of the bevel gauge intersects the base of the protractor exactly on center (*bottom photo*). Then either adjust the blade to the desired angle, or read the angle of the blade.

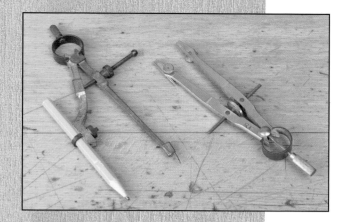

COMPASSES

A compass is useful in the shop for laying out circles and arcs. The most common types are the bow compass (*right in top photo*) and the wing compass (*left in top photo*). The bow compass is a drafting tool with a threaded shaft that runs between the legs held together with a spring on top. One leg holds a steel point, the other a pencil lead. The legs of a wing compass are hinged at the top or joined with a spring and forced open or closed by turning a knurled knob that attaches to a threaded post that spans the legs. One leg has a steel point and the other is often designed to hold a standard pencil.

Drawing circles

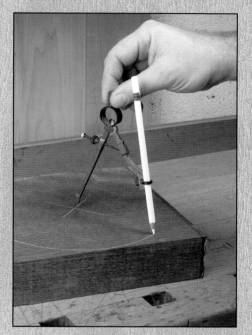

I like to set my compass with a steel rule. I set the steel point into the etched graduation at the 1" mark and then adjust the drawing point to the desired radius (plus 1"). Although the steel point of a compass generally does an adequate job of holding its place, I've found that making a slight starter hole with an awl helps keep the point from wandering as the compass is rotated to mark the circle or arc (*middle photo*).

Dividing circles

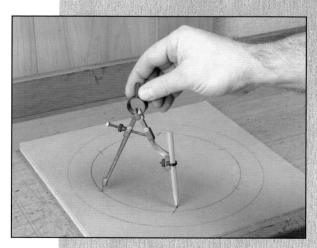

Here's a quick way to convert a circle to a hexagon or lay out six equally spaced holes (such as for spindles or mounting holes). With the compass still set to the desired radius, place the steel point on the perimeter of the circle and rotate the compass until it scribes a mark across the perimeter (*bottom photo*). Then move the steel point to this location and scribe another mark. Continue like this all the way around the circle—you'll end up where you started.

DIVIDERS AND CALIPERS

A spring divider differs from a compass in that both legs hold metal points instead of a single point and a pencil or pencil lead (*top photo*). The legs of the dividers are opened or closed by adjusting a knurled nut on one of the legs. Although you can use dividers to scribe circles or arcs, they are more commonly used for layout to "divide" (hence the name) or step out equal distances, often referred to as stepping off a measurement.

Stepping off measurements

Once you've set the dividers to the desired setting, you can easily "step off" equal measurements along a line by "walking" the dividers along the line. Simply pivot the dividers as you go by holding the post between your finger and thumb and moving the dividers from one point to another (*middle drawing*).

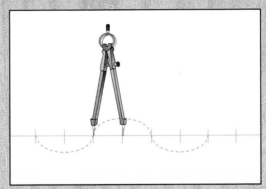

CALIPERS: INSIDE AND OUTSIDE

At first glance, a caliper looks very similar to a set of dividers. On closer examination you'll find that the difference lies in the legs. On a set of inside calipers, the legs bow in (*photo below right*); with outside calipers, they curve gently out at the ends (*photo at left*). Calipers are used primarily to take accurate inside and outside measurements so that these can be transferred to another layout or to reproduce a part. If you practice holding the caliper so that your fingers can adjust the knurled knob, you can set it with one hand, leaving the other hand free to steady the work.

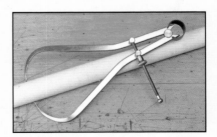

DIAL AND SLIDE CALIPERS

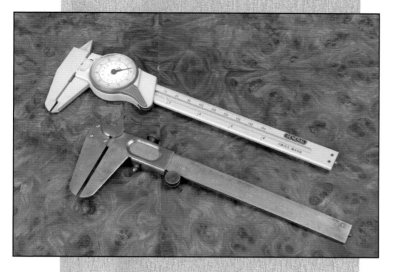

Thought of mostly as machinist's tools, dial and slide calipers can be quite useful in the woodworking shop. Although you rarely need to measure in thousandths of an inch, these precision tools are great for measuring small parts and checking the thickness of a workpiece. Slide calipers (*bottom caliper in top photo*) are not as easy to read as dial calipers (*top caliper in top photo*). Whoever came up with the idea of adding the dial deserves a medal, in my opinion. The bodies of slide calipers are usually metal, whereas you can find dial calipers with either metal or plastic bodies. The latest in calipers takes advantage of digital technology and offers a numeric readout (though these can be quite pricey).

Thickness

I've been using dial calipers for years to measure the thickness of stock (*middle photo*). I use one so regularly for this that it resides in my planer stand. Once you get used to using one of these, you'll wonder how you ever lived without it. Look for one with a dial that has 1/64" measurements as well as thousandths.

Depth gauge

Most dial and slide calipers can also be used as very accurate depth gauges. Just position the end of the caliper over the hole to be measured. Open the sliding jaw until the rod on the end of the caliper bottoms out in the hole; then read the dial (*bottom drawing*).

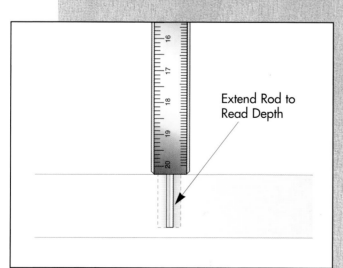

Extend Rod to Read Depth

CENTER FINDERS

Finding the center of a workpiece is a common layout task. It's so common that a number of tool manufacturers make plastic center finders, like the one shown in the top photo, specifically for this task. These simple tools have lips on two adjacent sides to quickly position the workpiece.

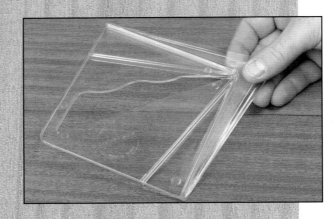

Basic use

To use a center finder like the one shown here, press the edges of the workpiece up against the lips of the center finder. Then butt a pencil or marking knife up against the center cutout and draw along this to mark a line on the workpiece. Next, rotate the workpiece 90 degrees and make another mark. Where the lines intersect is dead center (*middle photo*).

SHOP-MADE CENTER MARKER

In addition to finding the center of a workpiece, you'll often need to find the center on the edge of a board. The simplest and most accurate way I've found to do this is to make your own center marker. This is nothing more than a scrap of wood with a pair of dowels (or better yet, steel pins) and a hole in it for a pencil (*drawing at right*). The challenge is locating the pencil dead center. To do this, start by marking out and drilling the dowel holes (or use short lengths of 1/4" steel rod). Then install the dowels with glue (or epoxy for the metal rods). Now use these to locate dead center. Simply place a metal rule on edge between the dowels on a diagonal and make marks in both directions. Drill a hole for the pencil where the lines cross. (NOTE: For maximum accuracy, size this hole to accept a mechanical pencil.)

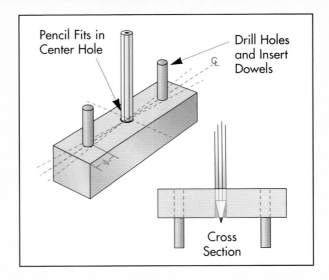

Pencil Fits in Center Hole

Drill Holes and Insert Dowels

Cross Section

Photo courtesy of
Bridge City Tool Works,
copyright 2001

TRAMMEL POINTS

Trammel points (also called a beam compass) come in handy when you need to draw a large-diameter circle or arc. Trammel points are a set of steel points that can be mounted on virtually any length beam, as long as it's straight (*top photo*). The heads are held in place by tightening a knurled knob on top of each trammel point. Some versions include an accessory head that accepts a standard pencil, in case you'd prefer a pencil line to a scribed line. Bridge City Tool Works (www.bridgecitytools.com) manufactures a gorgeous tool (*inset*) that features a beam with a built-in metal rule.

Basic use

Just like the panel gauge, trammel points require two hands for use. One hand holds one trammel at the pivot point, while the other hand moves the opposite head in a graceful arc or circle to mark the workpiece (*middle photo*). Keep the points razor-sharp and you'll need to apply only light pressure to mark your workpiece.

Stick trick

If you don't own a set of trammel points and need to draw a large-diameter arc or circle, try this crude but effective substitute. Simply drill a pair of small holes the desired distance apart in a thin stick. Use an awl or a brad to temporarily hold one end at the pivot point, and insert a pencil or awl in the other hole to scribe or mark the arc or circle (*bottom drawing*). Naturally, this isn't anywhere near as accurate as a good set of trammel points, but it'll do in a pinch.

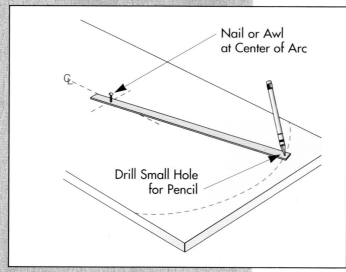

Nail or Awl
at Center of Arc

℄

Drill Small Hole
for Pencil

LARGE ARCS WITHOUT TRAMMELS

Sometimes, you may find that you need to draw a large arc that exceeds the ability of your trammel points, or that would require a really long beam, or you just don't have trammel points. In cases like these, try one of the variations of the old "bent stick" trick described below.

Bent stick

The boatbuilder adage "If it looks fair, it is fair" certainly applies here. Just grab a thin strip of wood that's long enough to create the desired arc, and have a helper flex the stick from start point to finish. Once the desired arc is obtained, draw along the wood strip with a pencil to mark it on the work-piece (*top photo*).

Plexiglass strip

One disadvantage to using a wood strip is the grain of the wood can and will affect how the strip flexes—often in an uneven arc. You can get around this if you've got some thin plexiglass handy. Since the plastic doesn't have any grain, any arc you flex in it will be perfectly smooth (*middle photo*).

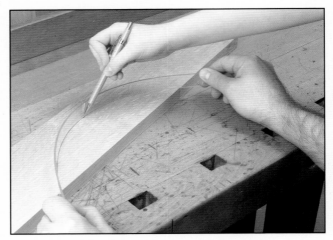

Clamp trick

It never seems to fail that whenever I need to use a bent stick to draw an arc, there's nobody around to help. When this occurs (and the arc is small enough), you can use a pipe clamp or bar clamp to flex the stick (*bottom photo*). This leaves your other hand free to transfer the arc to the workpiece.

DRAWING SMALL CURVES

If you're drawing-challenged, like me, you'll find a set of French curves a real boon when it comes time to lay out graceful curves for a project. French curves are available individually or in sets in a wide variety of shapes and sizes (*top photo*). Most are made of sturdy acrylic and may be clear or tinted. I prefer the clear curves, as this allows me to easily see the grain so that I can position the curves to maximize interesting grain patterns. French curves are available in most woodworking catalogs and at any art store.

Basic use

I most often use French curves to create patterns or templates (such as the cabriole leg shown in the middle photo). Slide the curve up and down along the workpiece until the desired curve is found. Then trace around the curve with a pencil or marking knife (I generally use a pencil, since a marking knife can cut and nick the plastic). French curves can also be used to lay out ovals (*inset*). Here again, position the curve until the desired shape is obtained, and trace around it. A pair of light pencil marks on the curve will help you align it for the remaining quadrants.

FLEXIBLE CURVES

A flexible curve is basically a lead rod that's covered with a vinyl sheath (*right photo*). This clever layout tool can be bent into small, graceful curves and is especially useful for reproducing a curve from an existing part, such as pressing it around a cabriole leg that you want to reproduce. Flexible curves can be found in most woodworking catalogs and at most any art store.

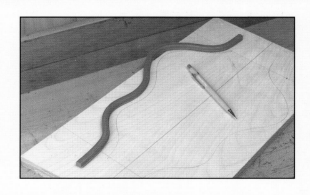

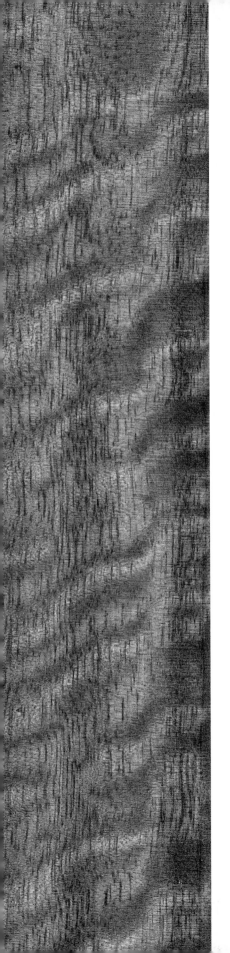

CUTTING TOOLS

In the 21st century, Mr. Disston is still correct. The shape and style of handsaws today—so basic and functional—have changed little from the time of this legendary sawmaker. His saws were (and still are) regarded as some of the best ever made: high-quality steel, easy to sharpen, and hold a keen edge. A Disston saw was meant to last a lifetime—and usually did.

The craft of fine handsaws has almost disappeared, certainly in mass retail. Go out and try to buy a quality rip saw, as I did just recently. After visiting five hardware stores, I came up empty. Unfortunately, the only handsaw in many shops now is a worn-out crosscut saw.

Why? Progress, of a sort: Most sawing operations have been taken over by power tools. That's too bad. In many cases, a quality saw in the hands of a skilled craftsman can produce results just as fine—but without the dust and noise. I'm not suggesting that you trash your power saws. But the next time you need to make just a cut or two, try a hand-powered saw. Mr. Disston would approve.

From top to bottom and left to right: a combined rip and crosscut handsaw made by Bissel & Moore Mfg. Co.; crosscut saw, 26", 12 point, made by Spear & Jackson, Sheffield; rip saw, 24", 3½ point, made by G. Collier, Brixton; rosewood and brass keyhole saw marked DIXON; and a small back saw with 7" blade, Henry Disston & Sons, Keystone Saw Works, Philadelphia.

SAW TERMINOLOGY

Before delving into the wide variety of saws available and their uses, it's important first to understand the terms used to describe saws, their teeth, and the cutting action.

Anatomy of a handsaw

Every saw has at least two parts: the blade and a handle (*bottom drawing*). Each blade generally has a toe (the end farthest from the handle) and a heel (the end closest to the handle). Handles may be open or closed (*see page* 42), intricate or simple, and be made of wood, metal, plastic, or a combination of these.

Saw teeth

For the most part, the configuration of the saw teeth will define whether the saw is designed to cut with the grain or against the grain. Teeth designed to cut with the grain are rip teeth, and are sharpened flat on the top to create a planing or chiseling action. Crosscut

teeth, on the other hand, are sharpened with fine points on the ends to act as small knives to cleanly sever the cross-grain wood fibers. Some saws are sharpened as sort of a hybrid, intended to be used for both crosscutting and ripping. These saws do a reasonable job, but not nearly as good as the individual saws.

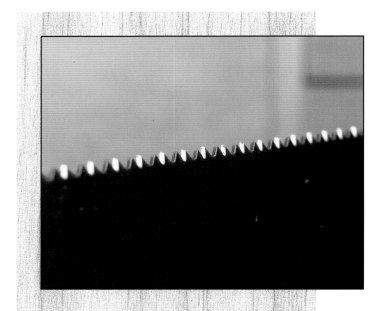

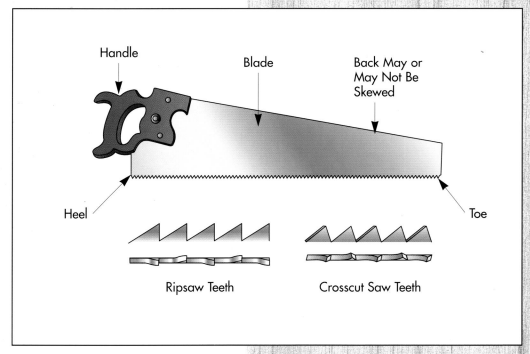

Handle

Blade

Back May or May Not Be Skewed

Heel

Toe

Ripsaw Teeth

Crosscut Saw Teeth

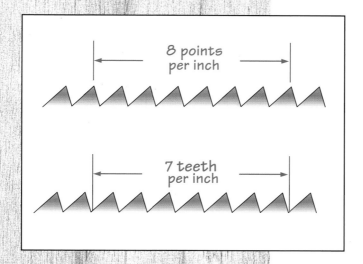

Teeth per inch

In addition to how a saw blade is sharpened, the number of teeth per inch will have a great impact on the performance of the saw. Generally, the greater the number of teeth, the finer the cut, and the longer it'll take to make the cut. There are two common systems used to describe this: teeth per inch and points per inch (*top drawing*). Points per inch includes the teeth at each point, whereas teeth per inch doesn't—a blade with 8 points per inch will have 7 teeth per inch.

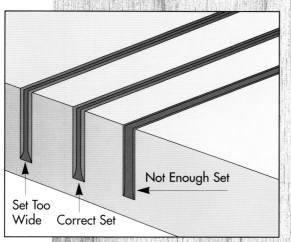

Kerf versus set

Another important characteristic of a saw blade is its set. Set is the amount each tooth is bent out from the saw blade. Without set, the blade would quickly bind in the kerf (*middle drawing*). Coarse-cutting saws (such as the rip saw) generally have a wider set than a finer cutting saw. This allows for plenty of clearance between the blade and the wall of the kerf. Aggressively set teeth are also commonly used on saws intended to cut green or wet wood. Here again, the wider set provides much-needed chip clearance.

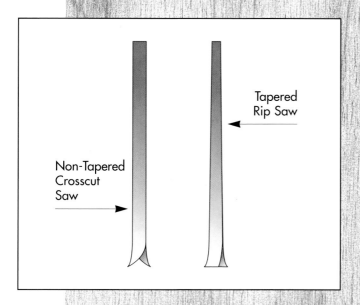

Tapered blades

Another common method used to prevent binding when cutting with a handsaw is to taper the blade (*bottom drawing*). Looking at a cross section of a tapered blade, you can see that the blade is a uniform thickness just above the teeth and then quickly begins to taper up toward the back. Most modern handsaws that you find in a hardware store or home center are not taper-ground—you generally have to pick up an older saw to find this useful feature.

Most handsaws have one of two handle styles: open or closed grip. Another common handle style is the turned or round handle common to coping, fret, and gent's saws. The type of grip you choose is a matter of personal taste. Whichever style you choose, go with a wood handle, as it's easy to shape and mold to fit your hand. It's surprising how many wood-workers are reluctant to modify a handle to better fit their hand. I always consider any "one size fits all" handle as a suggested starting point for shaping it to better fit my hand. Give it try: You'll be surprised what a big difference a custom-fit handle will make.

Open grip

An open grip (or pistol grip) can be found on some back and dovetail saws like the one shown in the top photo. I personally find this style of handle very comfortable, because it doesn't crunch my fingers like some closed grips do. If you've got large hands, you may find this grip more comfortable.

Closed grip

Closed grips are more common than open grips. They're generally more rugged and less easily damaged (*middle photo*). A closed grip saw also affords a slightly more rigid grip, especially if you frequently twist a saw to correct for a crooked cut.

26"

22 "

12 "

COMPARATIVE LENGTHS

Rip saws are generally the longest of handsaws, with crosscut saws the next longest. Shorter versions of crosscut saws (commonly referred to as panel saws) range between 20" and 22". Back saws average around 12" to 14" in length.

PROTECTING TEETH

For a saw to really function well, the teeth need to be sharp and stay sharp. Without some form of protection, the teeth can quickly dull if a saw is tossed into a toolbox or dropped into a tool well. Here are three simple ways to protect the teeth of your saws.

Garden hose

For large saws (like a crosscut or rip saw), the easiest way to protect the teeth is to cover them with a short length of garden hose (*top photo*). You can buy this by the foot at most home centers. Make a slit the full length of the hose with a utility knife, and slip it over the teeth. You may need to temporarily attach the hose to the saw blade with duct tape until the hose straightens out.

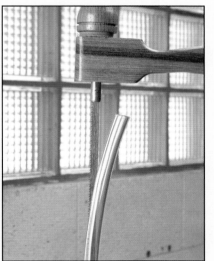

Plastic tubing

The teeth on smaller saws (like the bow saw shown in the middle photo) are best protected with smaller-diameter plastic tubing. Most home centers sell it by the foot. Just slit the tubing along its length and slip it over the teeth.

Report binders

For even smaller saws, such as a back or dovetail saw, the plastic spine from a report binder does a good job of protecting the teeth (*bottom photo*). These can be found at any office supply store and slip easily over the teeth.

RIP SAWS

A well-tuned rip saw is a joy to use. It's a shame that it's getting increasingly difficult to find a good rip saw at your local hardware store or home center. Fortunately, you can pick up a used rip saw at auctions, at estate sales, or on the Internet for just a couple of bucks. Rip saws are typically 26" in length and have around 5 teeth per inch (*top photo and inset*). Older saws feature a curved or "skew" back that was designed to reduce the weight at the toe, and reportedly improve the balance.

Teeth profile

A rip saw has chisel-like teeth that are designed to cut with the grain. In effect, they work like tiny planes or chisels to cleanly shear the wood fibers. The teeth are usually sharpened at around a 3-degree angle (*middle drawing*) and are flat at the top of the teeth to create the planing or chiseling action. Because most quality rip saws are taper-ground (*see below*), the set can be less aggressive.

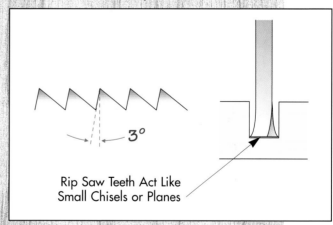

Rip Saw Teeth Act Like Small Chisels or Planes

Taper-ground

A quality rip saw will be taper-ground; that is, the blade will gradually decrease in thickness as it moves away from the teeth (*bottom drawing*). The area directly above the teeth is a constant thickness to provide solid support to the teeth. Tapering the blade greatly improves the clearance of the saw in the kerf, which reduces the likelihood of binding. This, of course, also makes it easier to drive the blade through the wood.

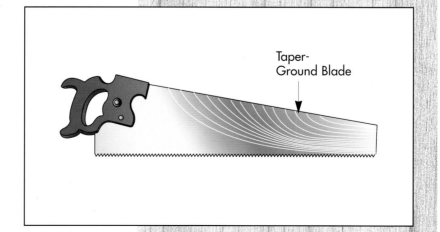

Taper-Ground Blade

The main reason many folks have difficulty ripping a board with a handsaw is that they're using a crosscut saw. A well-sharpened rip saw will slice through wood like a hot knife through butter. (For tips on starting a cut, *see page* 48.)

Beginning stance

With your hand, elbow, and shoulder all aligned with the saw blade, start your cut with the blade at a slight angle (*top photo*). This makes it easier to create a starting notch to guide the blade. Use your other hand to guide the blade at the start of the cut and to secure the workpiece as you continue.

Shift to a more vertical cut

To let the saw teeth do their job as tiny chisels or planes, it's best to shift to a more vertical cut as you make your way into the board (*middle photo*). Take long, even strokes and let the saw do the work. Concentrate on putting force into the downstroke, and lighten up on the upstroke. Try to keep a firm, relatively loose grip on the handle. As always, a well-sharpened saw will cut with little effort (*see pages* 184–185 *for details on sharpening a saw*).

Chatter

Anyone who has ever used a handsaw has probably experienced chatter—when the blade vibrates with a noisy chatter on the backstroke (*bottom drawing*). This is a sure sign of an alignment problem: You're most likely standing to one side or the other of the cut. The remedy is to keep saw, hand, elbow, and shoulder in the same plane.

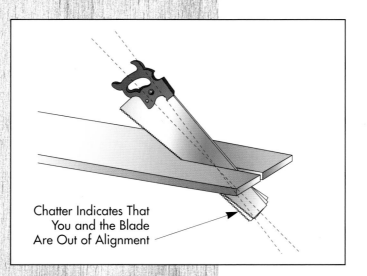

Chatter Indicates That You and the Blade Are Out of Alignment

CROSSCUT SAWS

A crosscut saw is designed to cut across the grain. Crosscut saws vary in length from 22" to 26" and generally have around 7 to 8 teeth per inch (*top photo*). Although you can find crosscut saws at most home centers and hardware stores, you may be better off picking up a used saw at an auction, estate sale, or garage sale. That's because the older saws were made with softer steel that allows for sharpening. Many of the modern saws use hardened teeth that are next to impossible to sharpen. Granted, they stay sharper longer; but when they do dull, you have to discard them. A quality older saw will last a lifetime with a little care and an occasional sharpening (*see pages 184–185 for more on this*).

Profile

The teeth of a crosscut saw act like tiny knives to cleanly sever the cross-grain wood fibers and to clear out the waste between the points (*middle drawing*). The teeth are usually sharpened at around a 14-degree angle and often have an aggressive set to prevent binding.

Bench hook anatomy

For accurate crosscutting (with any saw), I recommend using a bench hook. You can't find these in any catalog; you'll have to make your own. A bench hook is just a flat, wide piece of lumber with a pair of cleats fastened on the ends on opposite faces (*bottom drawing*).

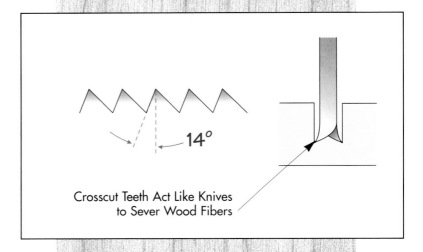

Crosscut Teeth Act Like Knives to Sever Wood Fibers

14°

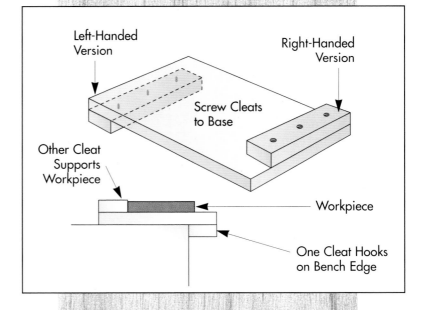

Left-Handed Version

Right-Handed Version

Screw Cleats to Base

Other Cleat Supports Workpiece

Workpiece

One Cleat Hooks on Bench Edge

Using a bench hook

A bench hook is positioned on the workbench so the cleat on the bottom hooks onto the edge of the workbench (*top photo*). The workpiece is butted up against the cleat on top, and slid over so the cut line aligns with the end of the cleat. This lets you use the cleat as a guide block to start the cut. The cleat also supports the wood fibers to help prevent splintering or tear-out.

Sight guide

Even with a bench hook, you may want to use some type of sight aid to help keep the saw blade vertical. A try square or engineer's square works well for this when you set it near the saw blade (*middle photo*). You can also use a known-square block of wood. Whichever you use, try to keep an even gap between the sight guide and the saw blade.

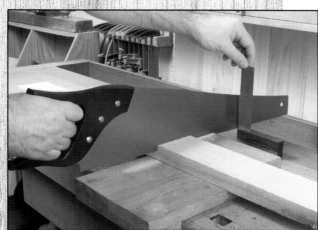

TOOLBOX SAWS

Toolbox saws are a modern invention that solves the age-old problem of trying to fit a full-sized handsaw into a tool box (note the size difference between the toolbox saw and handsaw shown in the photo at right). These short saws (typically around 16" long) fit in larger toolboxes and have aggressive teeth. Because of the aggressive teeth, they have limited use in the shop. They're suitable only for rough cuts, such as when rough-cutting boards to length.

STARTING A CUT

To make straight cuts with a saw, you have to start it straight. Sure, on saws with aggressively set teeth you'll be able to correct the cut somewhat; but you're always better off starting the cut straight in the first place. Here are three effective ways to accomplish this:

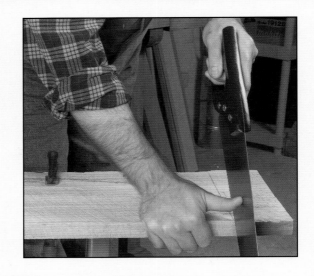

Finger as a guide

The classic way to start a saw cut is to use either a finger or your thumb as a guide (*top photo*). Start by marking a cut line on the board, then place the board on a sawhorse or clamp it to the bench. Next, use your thumb to guide the saw blade to the waste side of the cut. Try to keep the saw and your hand, elbow, and shoulder all aligned. Draw the saw back a few inches and make a series of short cuts to create a kerf. Keep the blade constantly pressed against your thumb as a guide.

Guide block

For added accuracy, you can start a cut with some type of guide block to hold the blade perpendicular to the work surface (*middle photo*). A guide block not only keeps the edge square, but it also helps make a straight cut across the board. Often hand pressure alone will work to hold the block in place, but it's better to clamp it to the board for stability.

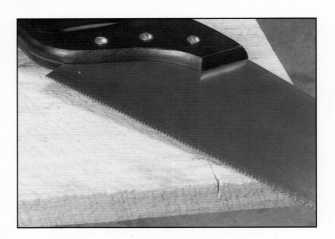

Starting notch

Regardless of the type of saw you're using, the surest way to prevent it from hopping off the intended mark is to make a starting notch (*bottom photo*). Just draw the saw back a few times to make a notch.

BACK SAWS

The back saw (also known as a dovetail saw) can be one of the most important hands tools in the shop. If you hand-cut joinery, a quality back saw can make a big difference. Back saws are identifiable by the brass or steel "back" that wraps around the top of the blade (*top photo*). This added rigidity allows for a thinner blade (typically around 0.030" thick), which creates a thin kerf and makes it easy to follow a pencil line or knife line.

Anatomy

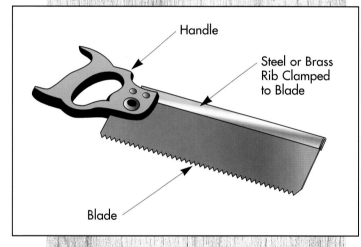

Handle

Steel or Brass Rib Clamped to Blade

Blade

Backs saws come in a variety of lengths ranging from 8" to 14" and have fine teeth (14 to 22 teeth per inch) that may be sharpened as crosscut, rip, or combination teeth. If you're planning on doing a lot of hand-cut joinery, it pays to get two back saws: one with crosscut teeth, the other with rip teeth. You'll find two predominant handle styles on back saws: open and closed (*middle drawing*). This really is a matter of personal preference; some woodworkers prefer the extra rigidity a closed handle offers over an open handle.

Basic use

Because the blade is so thin and the kerf is so fine, a well-sharpened quality back saw will generally steer itself in a perfectly straight cut—all you have to do is start the cut straight. Use a light grip on the saw and let it do the work (*bottom photo*). If you're using a saw that's sharpened as a crosscut to rip (such as when cutting the cheeks of a tenon), you'll get better results if you stop often to clean out the kerf and the saw teeth.

GENT'S SAW

A gent's saw (also referred to as a dovetail, blitz, or slotting saw) is a special type of back saw designed for extremely fine work (*top photo*). A further refinement of this saw is known as an offset dovetail saw (*inset*). This type of saw features an offset handle and blade that can be reversed to make it easy to saw close to a surface, such as when trimming a through tenon. Since the handle is not in line with the blade, I don't recommend this type of saw for cutting joints.

Anatomy

A gent's saw is usually much shorter than a standard back saw (4" to 10"), has finer teeth (20 to 33 teeth per inch), and typically has a turned handle in line with the blade

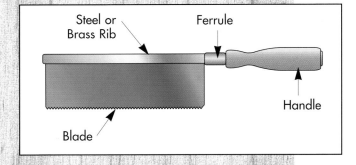

Inset photo courtesy of American Tool Companies, Inc., copyright 2001

(*middle drawing*). Usually there's a brass ferrule on the end of the handle to prevent the tang of the saw from splitting the handle over time. The teeth on a gent's saw are so fine that they're considered unsharpenable. When one of these gets dull, it's time to buy a new one.

Basic use

For the most part, a gent's saw should be reserved for use on small parts that require more delicacy than a back saw offers. They're great for fine detail work like cutting small rabbets, tenons, or dovetails (*bottom photo*). Because the blade is so thin and the kerf is so tight, the saw will cut straight as long as you start it straight. The only exception to this is a saw that's not set correctly (*see page 56 for more on this*).

Steel or Brass Rib   Ferrule

Handle

Blade

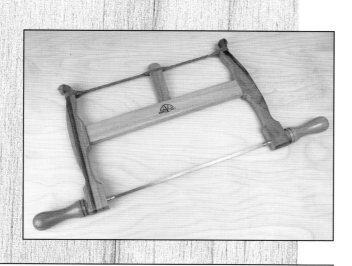

Bow Saws

If you've never used a bow saw, give it a try (*top photo*). It's amazing how versatile one of these can be. A bow saw can be used to rip, crosscut, or cut curves. Although found less and less in today's shop, you can still find them in the occasional woodworking catalog. The beauty of a bow saw is that the blades are interchangeable. You can install a wide rip blade for ripping, a narrower blade for crosscutting, or a fine blade for detail work.

Anatomy

A bow saw is a type of frame saw where the blade is held in an H-frame (*middle drawing*). Pins on the ends of the handles fit into holes in the ends of the blade. A stretcher connects to the cheeks of the frame via a loose mortise-and-tenon joint. Blade tension is provided by a twisted cord, cable, or threaded rod. The most common type of bow saw uses a toggle or twist stick to wind the cord to increase or decrease tension.

Basic use

Select the desired blade and install it in the saw. Adjust the twist stick to tension the blade. The grip that you use with a bow saw is really a matter of personal preference. Some folks like to place their hands on opposite cheeks of the frame. A more traditional grip is to hold a handle with one hand and then overlap your other hand over it so it also grips the frame. Others feel comfortable with just one hand guiding the saw (*bottom photo*).

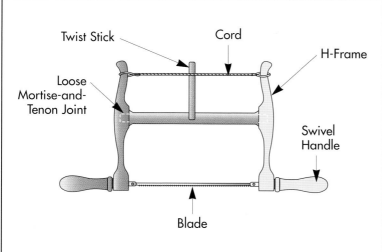

Twist Stick Cord H-Frame
Loose Mortise-and-Tenon Joint
Swivel Handle
Blade

COPING AND FRET SAWS

Coping and fret saws are yet other types of frame saws where the blade is held in a tensioned frame that is adjustable (*top photo*). Most coping saws accept a $6^5/_8$"-long, very thin, narrow blade with fine teeth—typically 15 to 32 teeth per inch. Fret saws often have deeper throats or an adjustable frame, and accept blades with extremely fine teeth: as high a 96 teeth per inch. Both coping saws and fret saws are terrific for cutting curves, making pieced cuts, and getting into tight places. Coping saws have the added feature of a blade that can be pivoted to make it easier to follow a curve.

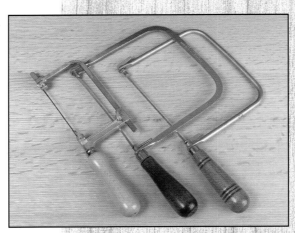

Anatomy

Blade tension for coping and fret saws is supplied by the steel frame. The blades are usually held in place with cross pins (although older coping saws may use blades with a hook or loop on the ends). These cross pins fit into grooves in metal spigots at the top of the frame and in the handle (*middle drawing*). The handle spigot threads into the handle and allows for fine adjustment of the tension.

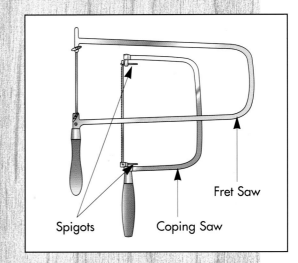

Spigots   Coping Saw   Fret Saw

Changing blades

To change the blade on a coping saw or fret saw, start by loosening the handle a few turns. Then position the saw upside down on your bench and press down on the handle slightly to "close" the frame (*bottom photo*). This creates sufficient slack in the blade so that you can slip the pin at one end of the blade out of the corresponding spigot. To install a blade, reverse the procedure. Insert the blade in one spigot, depress the frame, and slip the other pin in its matching spigot. Apply additional tension by tightening the handle.

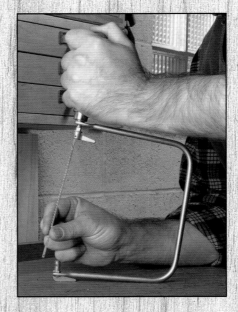

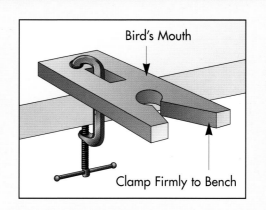

Basic use

In most cases, I install a blade so it cuts on the pull stroke. This does two things: It provides better control, and it keeps the blade in tension better than when pushing (*top photo and inset*). Since these blades are so thin and fragile, they have a tendency to overheat. There are a couple of ways to prevent this. First, use the full length of the blade as you cut. Second, stop periodically and allow the blade to cool.

Delicate cuts

For delicate cuts, such as cutting veneer or other thin materials for inlay or marquetry, the fret saw is the tool to use (*middle photo*). The extremely fine teeth let you negotiate curves without angling the blade. The secret to successful cutting is to fully support the thin material (*see the sidebar below*). Also, it's important to install the blade to cut down and on the pull stroke. This way, the cutting action pulls the material against the bird's mouth (*see the sidebar below*) instead of away from it, which would cause the thin material to fracture.

BIRD'S MOUTH

 The best way to support thin material when cutting with a fret saw is to use a V-notched board, called a bird's mouth, that clamps to your bench (*drawing at right*). The idea here is to position the workpiece and saw so that the cutting action takes place close to the point of the V for maximum support. For extremely accurate cuts, use the first few inches of blade nearest the handle, where the blade is the most rigid.

Bird's Mouth

Clamp Firmly to Bench

JAPANESE SAWS

If you haven't already tried one, Japanese saws are another one of those must-try tools (*top photo*). Unlike Western saws, which cut on the push stroke, Japanese saws cut on the pull. Many woodworkers (including myself) feel that this affords better control. Also, because the blade is pulled through the cut, there's less chance of crimping the blade. This means the blades can be thinner, which results in a thinner kerf. The metal used for Japanese saws is harder and the teeth are tempered to a high degree. This keeps them sharper longer, but makes them almost impossible to re-sharpen. This isn't a negative, since the tooth geometry is complex (*see the side-bar on page 55*), and with many of these you can replace the blade when it dulls.

Dozuki

Of all the Japanese saws, the dozuki (pronounced DOZE-oo-key) is my favorite. It's the Japanese equivalent of the Western back saw; and since I began cutting dovetails with one of these many years ago, it has earned a special place in my tool chest. Dozuki means "shoulder" in Japanese, and this saw was originally intended to cut the shoulders of a tenon. But I've found that this thin but rigid-backed blade is perfect for almost any hand-cut joinery (*middle photo*). Typically, this saw has around 26 teeth per inch and can vary from 8" to 12" in length.

Ryoba

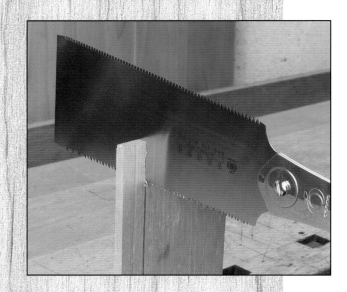

The ryoba saw (pronounced Ree-OH-bah) is a terrific saw to have on hand, as it combines the functions of a Western crosscut and rip saw in one tool (*bottom photo*). Ryoba means "double" in Japanese, and this saw has cross teeth on one side of the blade and rip teeth on the other. These saws come in blade lengths varying from 7" to 13". The smaller saw works well for joinery, and the larger versions are excellent for general-purpose cutting.

Azebiki

The azebiki saw (pronounced Eh-zeh-BEE-kee) is a special type of ryoba saw (crosscut teeth on one side, rip teeth on the other) that is designed specifically to make plunge cuts, such as a mortise or tenon in the center of a board (*top photo*). The blade is curved to let you easily start a cut in the middle of a workpiece. Its diminutive size makes it handy for getting into places other saws can't. The curved blade also makes it easy for you to clear sawdust from the kerf by simply using a rocking motion as you cut.

Kugihiki

The kugihiki saw (pronounced COO-gee-HEE-kee) is another specialty saw that you might find useful. In Japanese, kugi-hiki means "to cut nails," as in wooden nails or dowels. The super-thin blade does not have a back like the dozuki, so it's extremely flexible, but also prone to kinking. And just as important, the teeth on this style saw have no set. This means that the blade can rest on a surface without scratching it (*middle photo*). The downside to this is that binding can occur if you're removing a lot of wood, such as when cutting off a through tenon.

TOOTH PROFILES

If you examined the teeth of a Japanese saw with a magnifying lens, you'd find a complex tooth geometry—the teeth are longer and thinner and have more faceted surfaces than Western-style teeth (*drawing at right*). This is particularly true of the crosscut teeth. Unless you're willing to devote many hours to practicing sharpening these complex grinds, I suggest sticking with saws that have replaceable blades.

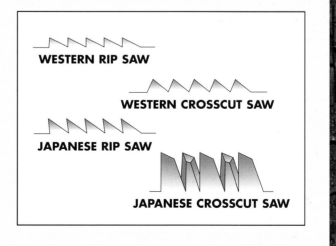

WESTERN RIP SAW

WESTERN CROSSCUT SAW

JAPANESE RIP SAW

JAPANESE CROSSCUT SAW

CHECKING FOR DRIFT

You've just bought a new back saw or dovetail saw, and after making a couple of test cuts, you notice they aren't straight. Is it you or the saw? Quite often it's the saw. In many cases the set of the teeth is too aggressive or not even. When this occurs, the saw tends to drift one way or the other. To eliminate this, use the procedure below.

Cut a kerf

Start by making a test cut in a scrap of wood. Hold the saw lightly, and don't try to compensate if it starts to drift off course. Let it make its own kerf (*top photo*).

Check for drift

Next, remove the saw from the kerf and check the kerf with a square (*middle photo*). Any deviation means that the teeth on one side either are set more aggressively or are sharper than the other side. This is also a good time to check for the overall set. Insert the blade back in the kerf and try to wiggle it; if there's a lot of slop, the set is too aggressive.

Correct the problem

To reduce the set on one side of the saw, use an oilstone. Set the saw on a flat surface and add a drop or two of honing oil to the stone and rub it gently over the teeth (*bottom photo*). If the overall set is too aggressive, do this to both sides, taking the same number of strokes per side. Take just a few strokes with the oilstone and make another test cut. Repeat as necessary until the saw no longer drifts and the blade doesn't wobble in the kerf.

SPECIALTY SAWS

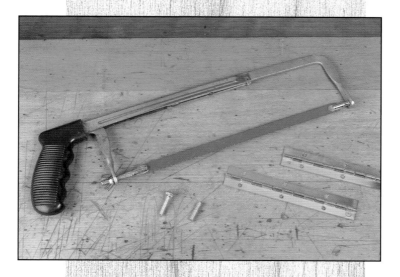

Hacksaw

A hacksaw in a woodshop? You bet. I often incorporate metal parts in many of the jigs, fixtures, and projects I build. And Murphy's Law says the carriage bolt or threaded knob I want to use will be too long. A hacksaw, with its fine teeth and hardened steel blade, will make short work of cutting through bolts, screws, even hinges (*top photo*). Choose blades with fine teeth for cutting through thin, hard metals and coarser teeth for softer materials like aluminum, which tend to clog the finer teeth.

Miter saw

For the most part, miter saws like the one shown in the middle photo have been replaced in the woodworking shop by the power miter saw. Miter saws are, naturally, designed to fit in a miter box; they're basically long back saws with crosscut teeth. If the blade is well sharpened and there's no play in the guides, this type of setup works well. Unfortunately, there's usually a problem with either the saw or the guides and so these can be used only for rough work.

Compass saw

The compass saw, or keyhole saw, has also generally been replaced by its electric cousins, the saber saw and jigsaw. Since this type of saw has no frame and a thin tapered blade, it can be used to make cuts where other saws can't (*bottom photo*). On the downside, with no frame and a thin, tapered blade, this saw is highly prone to bending and kinking in use. The only way to prevent this is to make light, non-rigorous cuts.

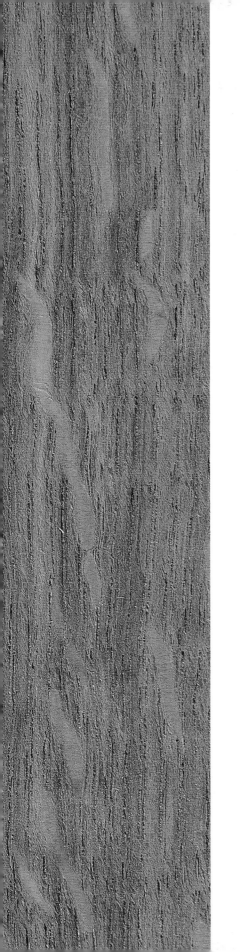

"You will see a surface change from dull to clear: rough-sawn or even machined it is dull and as you plane, it clears in little waves, the burnished patches are spreading like sunshine touching a field under scattered clouds."

JAMES KRENOV (1977)

SMOOTHING TOOLS

 Krenov is so poetically right here: Planing removes surface crud so that you can see the true beauty that lies beneath.

We've become brainwashed into thinking that our wood projects have to be as smooth as the artificial surfaces of plastic laminates like Formica. This is so sad, because wood offers such a rich, almost sensual surface. And this natural beauty is often obscured by power sanders.

Only hand-planing or scraping can produce the "burnished patches" we all appreciate. We glide our fingers over the well-worn edges of the table that Great Uncle Jasper made. We feel the irregularities—there's comfort here. We can feel the marks left behind by his tools—his honest work. So why do we try to conceal our own maker's marks? Because we've come to believe that smoothness without flaws is best. I don't buy it.

Leave your mark; let everyone know that you made this piece by hand. Revel in it. Let the wood have its character. It did come from a tree, after all, not from a plastic factory.

Clockwise from top left: a collection of Ohio Tool Company hand planes; Columbus, Ohio and Alburn, New York: No. 03, No. 05¼, No. 05¾, No. 06, No. 07 (in red), No. 08, No. 04½, No. 04¼, No. 02, No. 5, No. 5½, No. 03 (in center).

PLANE TERMINOLOGY

Hand planes are the workhorses of the woodworker's shop...and I'm not talking about the cabinetmakers of yesteryear. I'm talking about modern-day woodworkers who do fine, sensitive work. Anyone who knows me well can tell you that I don't get on a soapbox often. But the great "to sand or not to sand" debate is enough to get me going. I'm not a purist: I own and use power sanders. But I really love using my planes. And I reach for them whenever I can because, like Krenov, I truly believe they leave a superior surface.

It's sad to see so many woodworkers jump on the power sanding bandwagon as a standard way of woodworking. I've seen guys spend literally hours sanding out uneven surfaces or imperfections that could have been taken care of in minutes with a sharp plane. And to watch beautiful bird's-eye maple lose its crispness to sanding in place of a scraper plane just seems like a waste. Okay, enough ranting. If you have not had the pleasure of shearing off thin, wispy shavings from a board while working up a light sweat, I heartily recommend it.

The three types of planes you'll find most useful in the shop are jack or jointer planes, block planes, and specialty planes. Jack and jointer planes are used for smoothing panels, jointing edges, and all-purpose planing. Block planes, with their shorter soles and bevel-up blades, are great for trimming, fine-tuning joints, and planing end grain (*bottom drawing*). The bulk of the remaining planes you'll find handy are broadly classified as specialty planes. These include rabbet planes, shoulder planes, chisel planes, circular planes, combination planes, and so on.

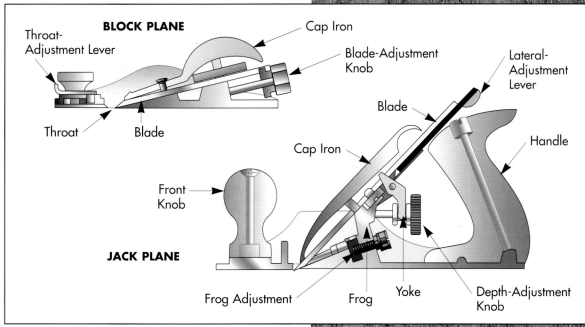

BLOCK PLANE

Throat-Adjustment Lever

Cap Iron

Blade-Adjustment Knob

Throat

Blade

Front Knob

JACK PLANE

Lateral-Adjustment Lever

Blade

Cap Iron

Handle

Frog Adjustment

Frog

Yoke

Depth-Adjustment Knob

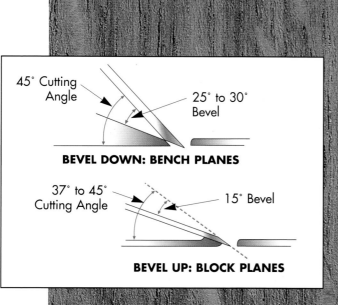

45° Cutting Angle

25° to 30° Bevel

BEVEL DOWN: BENCH PLANES

37° to 45° Cutting Angle

15° Bevel

BEVEL UP: BLOCK PLANES

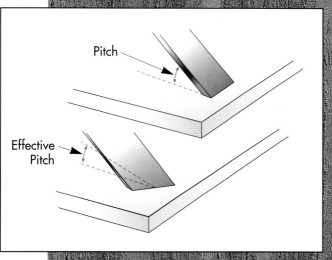

Pitch

Effective Pitch

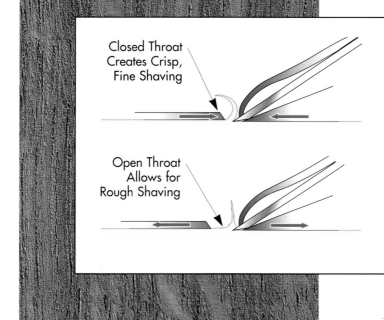

Closed Throat Creates Crisp, Fine Shaving

Open Throat Allows for Rough Shaving

Bevel orientation

One of the big differences between jack and block planes is the orientation of the bevel (*top drawing*). On a jack plane the bevel is down; with a block plane, it's up. Jack planes all have a chip breaker to help sever chips as they roll off the leading edge of the blade. Although a block plane looks like it doesn't have a chip breaker, the bevel actually serves this purpose. The blade on a block plane is also mounted much lower than that of a jack plane (roughly 25 versus 45 degrees). You might think this creates a much lower cutting angle, but it's actually roughly the same as the combined bevel plus mounting angle. This ends up around 45 degrees—the same as a jack plane (*to learn why a block plane handles end grain so well, see page 73*).

Skewing

Effective cutting angles can also be varied by skewing a plane. Instead of cutting straight in line, if you angle the plane, say, 30 degrees, you alter the effective pitch of the blade, as you're producing more of a shearing cut (*middle drawing*). This is why skewing is often used when working with hard-to-plane woods like bird's-eye maple or burls. Skewing is so effective, some plane makers manufacture their planes with skewed blades.

Throats

The throat opening on a plane—that is, the space between the beveled end of the blade and the sole—plays an important role in the tool's overall performance (*bottom drawing*). This sensitive area of the sole is the portion that "backs up" a cut. It prevents the blade from lifting up too large a sliver. At the same time, it must be wide enough to allow chips to pass through without jamming. The throat openings on jack and jointer planes are adjusted via a frog (*see page 67*), and on quality block planes they can be adjusted by adjustable throat plates (*see page 75*).

Jack and Jointer Planes

Traditionally, a craftsman's jack plane and jointer plane were his bread and butter. With these two planes, he could take a rough-sawn board and turn it into a straight board, smoothly surfaced on all four sides. The edges would be perpendicular to the faces, so the boards could easily be joined together to make larger panels. Although the electric jointer and planer have taken over these tasks in the modern shop, jack and jointer planes are still incredibly useful in the shop for surfacing a panel, jointing edges, and all-around smoothing. If you've never planed a rough-sawn board so that it's perfectly square, give it a try; you'll have a lot more respect for the cabinetmakers of the past.

Jack and jointer planes are very similar in appearance (*top photo*). The big difference is in the length of the sole and the width of the blade. Generally, the cutoff between a jack and a jointer plane is 18". Jointer planes begin around 22", and a mid-sized plane, often referred to as a fore plane, resides in the no-man's-land between the two (*see the chart below*). Another common rule of thumb is: The longer the sole, the wider the blade—but there are some exceptions to this.

Whether your plane is a jack, fore, or jointer,

PLANE SIZES

Sole	No.	Classification	Length	Cutter Width	Sole	No.	Classification	Length	Cutter Width
Metal	1	Smooth	$5^{19}/_{32}$"	$1^1/_2$"	Wood	23	Smooth	9"	$1^3/_4$"
Metal	2	Smooth	7"	$1^5/_8$"	Wood	24	Smooth	9"	2"
Metal	3	Smooth	8"	$1^3/_4$"	Wood	26	Jack	15"	2"
Metal	4	Smooth	9"	2"	Wood	27	Jack	15"	$2^1/_8$"
Metal	$4^1/_2$	Smooth	19"	$2^3/_8$"	Wood	$27^1/_2$	Jack	15"	$2^1/_4$"
Metal	5	Jack	14"	2"	Wood	28	Fore	18"	$2^3/_8$"
Metal	$5^1/_4$	Jack	$11^1/_2$"	$1^3/_4$"	Wood	29	Fore	20"	$2^3/_8$"
Metal	$5^1/_2$	Jack	15"	$2^3/_8$"	Wood	30	Jointer	22"	$2^3/_8$"
Metal	6	Fore	18"	$2^3/_8$"	Wood	31	Jointer	24"	$2^3/_8$"
Metal	7	Jointer	22"	$2^3/_8$"	Wood	32	Jointer	26"	$2^5/_8$"
Metal	8	Jointer	24"	$2^5/_8$"	Wood	33	Jointer	28"	$2^5/_8$"
Wood	21	Smooth	7"	$1^3/_4$"	Wood	34	Jointer	30"	$2^5/_8$"
Wood	22	Smooth	8"	$1^3/_4$"					

it will have similar parts. Older planes had wood bodies or soles, and modern planes have metal bodies. For a short while, "transitional" planes were made that supposedly offered the best of both worlds. (*For more on this, see page 72.*)

One of the best ways to get familiar with a jack plane or jointer plane is to take one apart. Start by loosening the cap lock to release its pressure (*bottom drawing*). Then slide the lever cap up and off the screw. Now you can lift out the

blade and cap-iron assembly. These two pieces are held together by a screw that can be loosened with the lever cap or a wide-blade screwdriver. Twist the cap iron, slide it over until it slips over the screw, and lift it off. The cap iron (also called a chipbreaker) helps sever chips as they are lifted up by the blade; it also serves as a stiffener to help prevent chatter.

The cap iron and blade fit onto the frog—a separate casting that's screwed to the body of the plane. On better planes, there's an adjustment screw in the rear of the frog that allows you to move the frog to open or close the throat opening. The frog also houses the lateral-adjustment lever that aligns the blade parallel to the sole, and the depth-adjustment knob that raises or lowers the blade. A wood handle on the back and a knob on the front complete the plane.

The blades may be sharpened in one of three common ways: straight, convex, or with softened corners (*top drawing*). Convex is useful for rough work, and softening the corners helps prevent them from digging in.

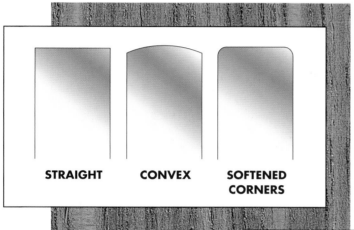

STRAIGHT   **CONVEX**   **SOFTENED CORNERS**

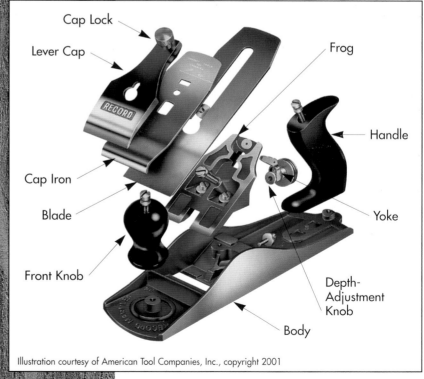

Cap Lock

Lever Cap

Frog

Handle

Cap Iron

Blade

Yoke

Front Knob

Depth-Adjustment Knob

Body

Illustration courtesy of American Tool Companies, Inc., copyright 2001

TUNING A HAND PLANE

For a jack plane or jointer plane to create thin, wispy shavings without tear-out, you'll need to tune it. This involves flattening the sole, adjusting the frog, removing any slop in the cap iron, sharpening the blade, and fine-tuning the lateral and depth adjustments.

Flattening the sole

The flatness of a plane's sole will have a huge impact on its performance. The easiest way to check a sole for flatness is with a straightedge. I've found that holding the plane up against a bright light while doing this will best show any dips or high spots.

To flatten a sole, temporarily fasten some sheets of silicone-carbide sandpaper to a known-flat surface with spray adhesive. A piece of replacement glass for a Jalousie window works great (available at most hardware stores). What's really nice about Jalousie glass is that its edges are rounded-over for safety. I usually start with 80-grit and work my way up to 220-grit.

Although you might be tempted to remove the blade and cap iron, don't—they keep tension on the sole. If you flatten it without this tension, and then install the iron, the sole won't be flat. Just make sure to back off the iron 1/8" or so before rubbing the sole on the silicon-carbide paper. Use firm, steady strokes, and flip the plane end-for-end occasionally to ensure even pressure over the entire length and width of the sole (*top photo*). Check the sole often for progress. Although purists will flatten the entire sole, the only parts where it's critical that it be flat are the toe, heel, and around the throat (*middle photo*).

The frog

The frog is another important part of the plane. It holds the plane iron firmly at the proper angle, while at the same time letting you adjust the depth of cut and the position of the

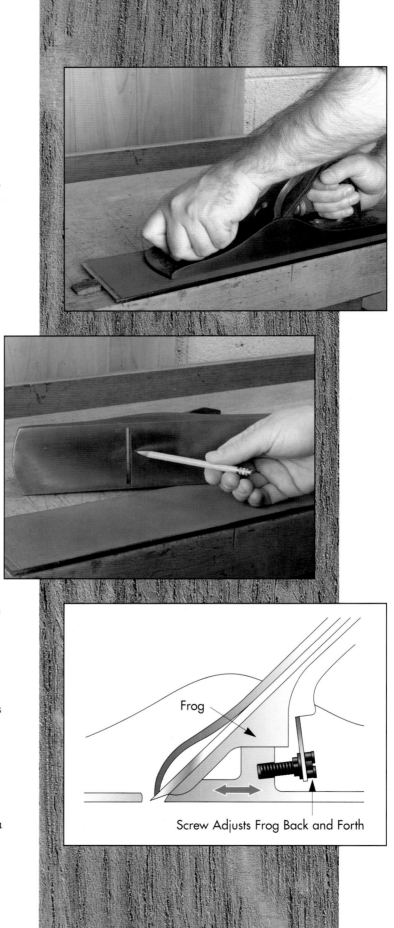

Frog

Screw Adjusts Frog Back and Forth

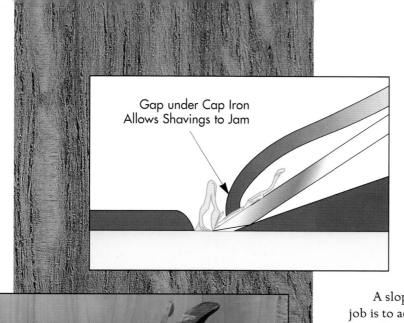

Gap under Cap Iron Allows Shavings to Jam

iron (*bottom drawing on opposite page*). A poorly tuned frog is the leading cause of blade chatter. For a frog to do its job well, its mating surfaces— the bottom where it contacts the sole, and the sloped face that holds the plane iron—must be absolutely flat and square. To flatten these, I use a diamond hone or a small stone and gently rub it on the surface. Check often with a straightedge.

Cap iron

A sloppy cap iron can also cause chatter. Its job is to add rigidity to the plane and prevent it from flexing. The slight hump at the end also serves as a wedge to break chips as the iron cuts into the wood. Neither of these will happen if the cap iron doesn't fully contact the entire edge of the plane iron. And a poorly fitting cap iron can allow shavings to jam up between the cap iron and the blade (*top drawing*). The solution to all these problems? Ensure full contact by flattening the front edge of the cap iron on an oilstone.

Before you attach the cap iron to the blade, the blade needs to be sharpened. (*For an in-depth look at sharpening, see pages* 182–183.) Then re-attach the cap iron and secure it to the blade to check for gaps (*middle photo*). Position the cap iron on the blade square to the front edge and set back about $^1/_{16}$".

Handle and knobs

If the handle and knobs of the plane are in good shape, take a moment to tighten the screws that secure them to the plane body. There's usually one for the knob and two for the handle (*bottom photo*). If the handle is cracked or broken, replace it with a new one (*see the sidebar on page* 66).

Depth of cut

If you removed the frog, you'll need to fine-tune it. Start by loosening the frog screws so they're friction-tight (*top photo*). Then, use the frog-adjustment screw to slide the frog to align with the sole at the throat opening. You may need to remove the handle to get to this screw. NOTE: If there's a lot of play in the depth-adjustment knob, you may be able to remove the slop. If the yoke that accepts the knob is steel or brass, you can squeeze it tighter with a C-clamp. If the yoke is cast, leave it alone—any pressure at all will likely snap it.

Lateral adjustment

There's not much to do on the lateral-adjustment lever; check for burrs on the cam, and smooth any you find with a fine file or a piece of emery cloth. Then flip the plane over and sight down along the sole. Pivot the lateral-adjustment lever back and forth until the edge of the plane blade is parallel with the sole (*middle drawing*).

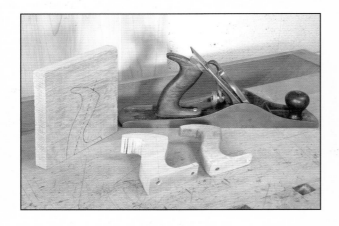

CUSTOM HANDLES

■ To make a new handle, use the old handle as a template (*left photo*). It's best to drill the hole for the handle screw before shaping the handle. Then cut out the shape, and smooth and sand the handle to fit your hand. Even if there's nothing wrong with your handle (or the front knob), I always suggest shaping them to fit your hand. The factory-made handle is designed to fit the "average" hand, not yours. A custom-fit handle feels much better.

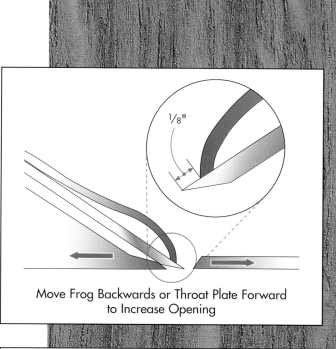

Move Frog Backwards or Throat Plate Forward
to Increase Opening

Move Frog Forward or Throat Plate Backwards
to Decrease Opening

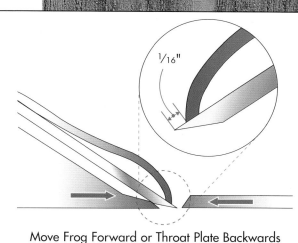

USING A JACK PLANE

Once your jack plane or jointer plane is well tuned, there's one more thing to do before you use it: You need to adjust it to match the type of cut you're making. I'm not talking about depth of cut here, but the position of both the cap iron and the frog.

Rough cuts

For rough cuts, such as preliminary surfacing of a board, you'll want to adjust the cap iron to allow for a fairly heavy shaving (*top drawing*). Loosen the cap iron screw and shift the cap iron so it's about 1/8" away from the cutting edge. Then loosen the frog screws and turn the frog-adjusting screw to increase the throat opening. This lets you take thicker, coarser shavings without jamming.

Smooth cuts

For smooth or finish cuts, it's well worth the effort to readjust the plane. Many woodworkers fail to realize the importance of the cap iron and frog position for these crucial cuts. The goal is to move the cap iron closer to the cutting edge of the blade so that it will quickly break chips and prevent tear-out (*middle drawing*). At the same time, adjust the frog to close the opening. This still allows the finer shavings to pass through while affording better support to the wood fibers being severed.

Pencil tip

Now you're ready to plane. But before you do, consider this simple tip to help you clearly see where you have and haven't planed. Rub the lead of a pencil lightly over the edge or face of your workpiece (*bottom photo*). As you plane, you'll be able to readily check your progress.

Hand-planing is hard work: enjoyable, but it requires physical effort. If you've ever tried planing a board with arm strength alone, you learned quickly that planing is a whole-body task. Your legs are just as important as your arms. Take a stance centered on the board, where your legs are spread a bit wider than your shoulders, with knees slightly bent (*top photo*). Though you'll want to maintain firm, even pressure on the plane, take care to hold the knob and handle with a light grip: If you use a "white-knuckle" grip, your hands will quickly tire.

Start the cut

Before you begin to plane a board, take a moment to "read" the grain. Look at the edge of the board, and clamp it to the bench so that the grain will be sloping down and toward the body of the plane. Set the plane on the workpiece so the body extends off the board with the blade just in front of the leading edge of the board (*middle drawing*). Press down firmly on the front knob, and push the handle steadily with your other hand.

Complete the cut

As the plane passes over the end of the board, continue to press down on the knob while pushing forward and down on the handle (*bottom drawing*). As the blade nears the end of the board, lessen the pressure on the knob and concentrate on pressing down on the handle as you continue to push the plane forward.

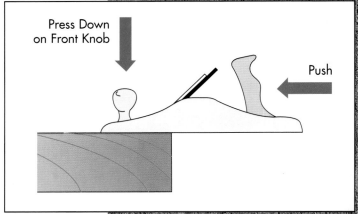

Press Down on Front Knob

Push

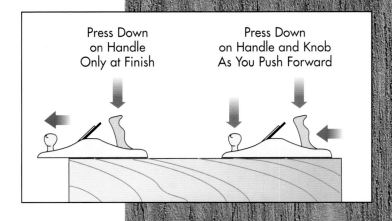

Press Down on Handle Only at Finish

Press Down on Handle and Knob As You Push Forward

Smoothing a Panel

One of the most frequent reasons I reach for my jack plane is to smooth a panel that's been glued up from several boards. Even with careful prep and clamping, there is almost always an edge that needs to be knocked off or smoothed out.

Skew cuts

To quickly remove high spots, skew the plane at a slight angle (*top photo*). Skewing the plane also produces more of a slicing cut and has less of a tendency to tear-out. The disadvantage to skewing is that you effectively shorten the body; this means it will follow surface undulations instead of removing them.

Go with the grain

As mentioned earlier, you always want to plane with the grain to avoid chipping and tear-out (*middle photo*). Although this sounds simple, it can be a real challenge, depending on the wood. The grain pattern on any single board can (and often will) change direction over its length. This is compounded in a panel glued up of several boards, where the grain direction can be haphazard. Take the time to read the panel carefully, and make pencil marks directly on the panel indicating grain direction. Alter your planing to compensate.

Light finish cut

Once the panel is flat, adjust the plane for a fine cut (*see page 67*) and then take a series of light passes over the entire surface to create a panel as smooth as a baby's bottom (*bottom photo*).

USING A JOINTER PLANE

The long body of a jointer plane makes it the ideal plane for flattening boards. Unlike shorter-bodied planes that would ride up and down in the hollows and high points on a board's surface, a jointer plane will span these hollows and will quickly knock off the high points to produce a flat surface (*top drawing*).

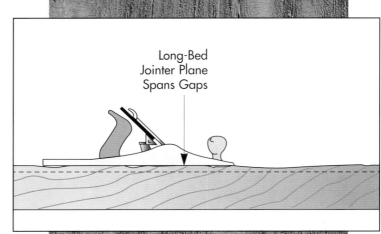

Long-Bed Jointer Plane Spans Gaps

Basic use

The general rule of thumb for planes is, the longer the body, the wider the blade. This means that larger jointer planes are capable of taking a large "bite" out of the wood surface. To prevent this, it's important to keep the blade razor-sharp and take light cuts (*middle photo*). Note that when you first start leveling a board, it will probably feel like you're not removing much wood—and you won't be. All you're doing at the beginning is lopping off the high spots. As they level out, you'll find the plane taking bigger shavings. As with a jack plane, this will require considerable physical effort. It's important to keep a firm but relaxed grip, and use your entire body, not just your arms.

Upside down

If you flip your jointer plane upside down and clamp it in your bench vise, you'll find that you've created a miniature hand-powered version of an electric jointer (*bottom photo*). This is handy for planing long, flat edges on thin or narrow stock, or any workpiece that would be difficult to clamp in a vise for planing. Use steady, even pressure, and skew the workpiece slightly to produce more of a slicing cut.

I've always found that jointer planes do a better job of flattening or smoothing thin stock than smaller planes. That's because the long body of the plane often applies pressure over the entire length of the workpiece when planing. This helps prevent the thin workpiece from buckling under planing pressure. For really thin stock, I temporarily attach the wood to a flat base (typically MDF) with double-sided carpet tape (*top photo*). Cover the entire underside with tape—any gaps can allow the stock to deflect, resulting in a scalloped cut. ShopTip: To free the thin, delicate stock from the base afterwards, drizzle some lacquer thinner on the base and let it seep under the workpiece. The lacquer thinner will dissolve the adhesive, letting you pull up the thin stock without breaking it.

Edge-jointing

One of my favorite uses for a jointer plane is to joint edges of boards to be glued up (*middle photo*). There's just something truly satisfying about watching a 4- or 5-foot continuous shaving curl out of the top of the plane. One of the challenges here is that you need to walk along with the plane as you work. The trick is to keep your elbows locked at the same height as you move your body alongside the plane. With a little practice you'll find that this is a very natural motion.

LOW-ANGLE PLANE

■ Patterned after the Stanley No. 62 low-angle plane, the low-angle jack plane shown here is manufactured by Lie-Nielsen Toolworks, Inc. (www.lie-nielsen.com). It's sort of a hybrid of a low-angle block plane and a jack plane. It took only a few passes with this beauty for me to realize it would become one of my favorite planes. It works extremely well on squirrelly and troublesome grain, and I've even used it to plane the end grain when making raised panels with no shoulder.

WOOD AND TRANSITIONAL PLANES

■ Before metal-bodied planes became the norm, wood and wood/metal hybrids known as "transitional" planes were the standard. Although you can still find some modern wood planes, most wood and transitional planes are antiques, gathering dust on shelves. That's too bad, because there are plenty of shavings left in these classic tools.

Wood-body planes

The advantage a wood-bodied plane offers over a metal plane is more aesthetic than technical (*top photo*). Some woodworkers (including me) appreciate the warmth and natural feel that a wood sole offers. And it seems less harsh to the workpiece. The downside to a wood sole is that wood moves. Wood-bodied planes need continuous attention to ensure the sole is flat; fortunately, it's a lot easier to true up then a metal sole. Additionally, adjusting the blade is cumbersome.

Transitional planes

Transitional planes were designed to bridge the gap between wood-bodied and metal planes. They combined a wood sole with the convenient blade adjustments of a metal plane (*middle photo*). I tuned up my great-grandfather's old Stanley No. 132 jointer plane years ago. Although it's a bit finicky, I use it all the time.

Blade adjustment

The big difference between a wood plane and a transitional plane is how the blade is adjusted (*bottom drawing*). On a wood plane, the blade is held in place with a wedge. Tapping the heel or toe of the plane raises or lowers the blade, respectively. With transitional planes, the blade rests on a metal frog and is adjusted up and down by a knob or lever.

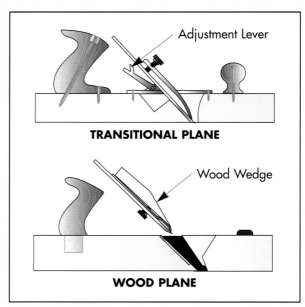

Adjustment Lever

TRANSITIONAL PLANE

Wood Wedge

WOOD PLANE

BLOCK PLANES

Of all the hand planes in my shop, the one I reach for most often is my block plane. That's because it's so handy for fitting joints, trimming parts, and planing a delicate detail like a chamfer or roundover on a table top. Block planes typically run between 5" and 6½" in length and were originally designed to plane ornery end grain (*top photo*). Many woodworkers mistakenly believe that the reason a block plane handles end grain so well is that the blade is at a much lower angle than a standard plane's. True, the blade is much lower (roughly 20 versus 45 degrees for a standard bench plane), but the effective angle is virtually the same. Why? The blade on a block plane is installed bevel up instead of bevel down (as on a standard plane). When you add the typical 25-degree bevel that's ground onto the blade to the 20-degree blade angle, you end up at 45 degrees.

So why does a block plane work better on end grain? First, the lower blade angle allows for a one-handed grip that puts the hand, elbow, and shoulder in line—this creates a much more effective thrust. Second, since the bevel is up (and there's no need for a frog), the blade can rest firmly on the bed of the body, so it's fully supported virtually all the way up to the cutting edge (*bottom drawing*). This excellent support, combined with an efficient stroke, allows a block plane to cleanly sever wood fibers without chatter or tear-out.

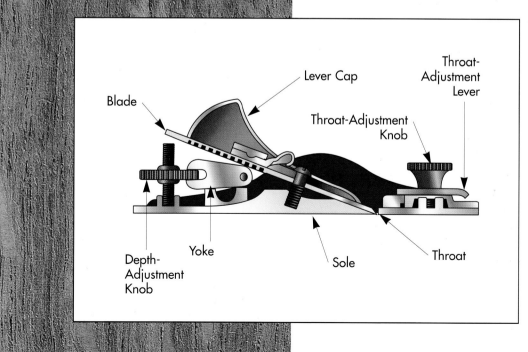

Blade · Lever Cap · Throat-Adjustment Lever · Throat-Adjustment Knob · Depth-Adjustment Knob · Yoke · Sole · Throat

There are two main types of block planes available today: a standard block plane and a low-angle block plane. As discussed earlier, the blade on a standard block plane rests on the body at about 20 degrees—this creates an effective angle of 45 degrees (*top drawing*).

Low-angle block plane

The blade on a low-angle block plane rests on the bed at about 12 degrees (*middle drawing*). Combined with a 25-degree bevel, this yields an effective cutting angle of approximately 37 to 38 degrees. You wouldn't think that 12 degrees would make much difference, but it does. I've found that a well-sharpened low-angle block plane will generally outperform its higher-angle cousin. My block plane of choice is the Record 60½. It fits well in both my apron pocket and my hand. If you have smaller hands, you may find the Stanley 60½ more to your liking; it's about ¼" narrower than the Record.

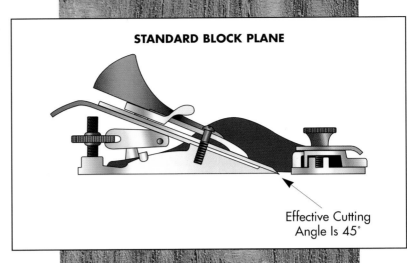

STANDARD BLOCK PLANE

Effective Cutting Angle Is 45°

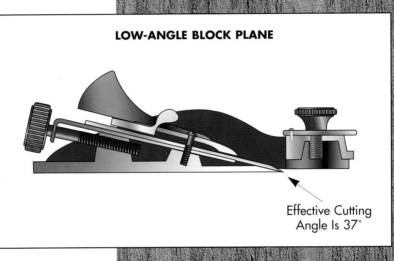

LOW-ANGLE BLOCK PLANE

Effective Cutting Angle Is 37°

KNUCKLE-JOINT BLOCK PLANES

■ An interesting aside to the evolution of the block plane is the knuckle-joint plane, introduced by Stanley in 1888. Virtually identical to a Stanley No. 9, these block planes had a longer lever cap screw and a unique hinged lever cap known as the knuckle joint. This plane was designed to provide a more comfortable one-handed grip. The smooth top of the cap, along with the absence of a protruding mechanism, helps this plane nest comfortably into the palm of your hand. If you're fortunate enough to stumble across one at a yard sale or auction (and the price is right), snap it up.

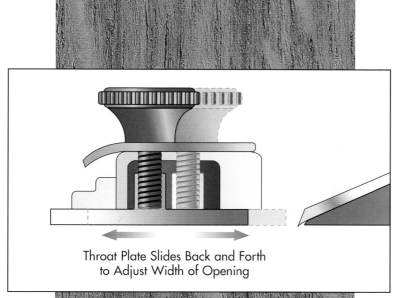

Throat Plate Slides Back and Forth
to Adjust Width of Opening

Adjustable throat

Since they have no frog to adjust the blade back and forth to open and close the throat opening, some block planes offer an adjustable throat plate (*top drawing*). This lets you close the opening for fine cuts, and open it for coarser work. Inexpensive "hardware-store" variety block planes do not have adjustable throats. In my opinion, they're not worth the money. For just a little more, you can pick up a quality block plane that has an adjustable throat. To adjust the opening, loosen the lock knob and pivot the lever to move the plate open or closed.

Depth adjustment

Another feature to look for in a block plane, in addition to an adjustable throat, is a depth-adjustment mechanism. You want one that works well and is comfortable. The middle photo shows three common methods for adjusting depth. At top in the photo is a standard block plane with a horizontal "disc" or wheel that's turned to raise or lower the blade. Below this is my personal favorite (common on low-angle block planes), an in-line knurled knob that's rotated to adjust depth. And finally, even though it's a nuisance to adjust, I've got a wood-body block plane that feels nice in my hand (*bottom plane in middle photo*); to adjust the depth, you tap on the metal cap on the back of the body to raise the blade, and on the front of the body to lower the blade.

Grips

There are three common grips I use with a block plane: light, heavy, and reverse. The grip I use most is the light grip (*bottom photo*). The plane nestles in the hand while the fingers wrap around it with the index finger pressing down on the throat-plate lock knob. This grip works well for most trimming and fine-tuning jobs.

Although I don't often use a block plane to remove a lot of wood, a heavier grip comes in handy every now and then. For this grip, I use two hands to guide the plane (*top photo*). This works especially well when planing end grain, since you want firm pressure to prevent chatter.

Reverse grip

Just like a Japanese plane (*see page* 92), you may find that you have more control over a block plane if you reverse it in your hand (*middle photo*). This grip lets you pull the plane instead of pushing it. I often use this grip when chamfering edges or making a final pass on an edge of a workpiece.

A hybrid of the heavy and reverse grips is to use both hands to pull the plane. One hand grasps the throat-plate lock knob to pull the plane, while the other hand wraps around the body of the plane in a reverse grip to guide it through the cut. If you skew the plane body slightly, you'll find that this modified grip works extremely well on end grain.

A PLANE "KIT"

■ I bought my first plane when I was 14. It was a knockoff of a Stanley No. 4½ that I picked up at Warner's hardware store in downtown Minneapolis. Man, was I excited to get home and use it. After I pulled it out of the box and clamped a piece of scrap wood to my bench, I gleefully made my first pass. Ugh! What a disappointment—it tore up the edge, and shavings jammed up under the blade and cap iron. Must be me, I thought: Maybe I'm not using it right or I don't have it adjusted properly.

As you might suspect, this was my first lesson in the school of hard knocks on hand tools, particularly planes. What I'd really purchased was a plane "kit." Little did I know then that an afternoon of "tweaking" would have produced a tool capable of creating perfect shavings.

My point is, almost every plane you buy needs some serious fine-tuning before it will function properly. Fortunately, this isn't difficult (*see pages 64–66 for tuning a jack/jointer plane and pages 77–78 for tuning a block plane*). As a matter of fact, you may find it quite enjoyable. It's a great way to spend a rainy afternoon in the shop.

TUNING A BLOCK PLANE

Since a block plane is often used to plane end grain and other hard-to-plane wood like twisted or squirrelly grain, it's imperative that the plane be tuned accordingly. This involves flattening the sole, sides, and bed under the iron, adjusting the throat, sharpening the blade, and tuning the lever cap.

Flatten the sole

Although a flat sole for a block plane isn't as critical here as it is for the longer-bodied planes, it's still important to ensure full support around the blade (*top photo*). Just as with a longer plane (*see page* 64), the key points that need to be flat are the toe, the heel, and around the throat opening. The area around the throat opening is the biggest concern, since this is the area that will ensure solid support for the blade as it cuts.

Flatten the sides

Since block planes are occasionally used on their sides, it's a good idea to check them to make sure they're 90 degrees to the sole. Use a small engineer's square for this; if you find any deviation, flatten the sides as you did the sole (*middle photo*). Stop often and recheck with the square. At the same time, I like to soften the edges of the sole by filing a slight ($1/16$") chamfer all the way around the body. This makes the plane fit more comfortably in my hand and helps prevent dings on the workpiece.

The bed

The bed that the plane iron rests on is rarely flat, and this is a leading cause of chatter in a block plane. The best way I've found to flatten it is with a paddle-style diamond hone like the one shown in the bottom photo. Use firm pressure to keep the paddle flat, and continue honing until the bed is flat over its entire surface.

Throat opening

If you're fortunate enough to have an adjustable-throat block plane, you can fine-tune the throat opening by loosening the adjustment knob and pivoting the lever to open and close the opening (*top photo*). The mating surfaces of the adjustable throat plate and plane body will also benefit from a stroke or two by a diamond hone.

Sharpen the blade

A razor-sharp blade is essential for a block plane to do its best. I generally grind a hollow bevel on the blade and then hone a microbevel (*middle photo*). *See pages 182–183 for detailed instructions on sharpening a plane blade.*

Fine-tune the lever cap

The lever cap on a block plane combines the functions of the cap iron and the lever cap on a larger plane. It has to press the blade securely into the plane body (while still allowing for adjustment), and it has to hold it rigid to prevent chatter.

Here again, it's imperative that the front edge of the lever cap make full and continuous contact with the plane blade. The best way to ensure this is to flatten the edge on an oilstone (*bottom photo*). You'll need to experiment a bit to find the optimal angle; hone a little and then reassemble the plane. Check for gaps by trying to slip a feeler gauge between the lever cap and the blade.

USING A BLOCK PLANE

End grain

Even though block planes are designed to handle difficult end grain, you still have to be careful when you're planing near an edge. That's because the unsupported end grain near the end of a board will easily splinter and chip out. Fortunately, there are a couple of simple ways to prevent this.

Plane toward the center

One common method to prevent chip-out when planing end grain is to plane only toward the center of the board (*top photo*). This way, all the wood fibers are supported by the fibers in front of them. Simply plane about halfway from one side, then reverse the plane direction and plane from the other side. The downside to this method is it can be difficult to create a truly flat surface. I generally reserve this for detail work such as planing a slight chamfer on a table top.

Support the end with a scrap

A more reliable way to prevent chip-out is to clamp a waste or "sacrificial" piece to the end of the board you're planing (*middle photo*). This fully supports the end grain and permits a full stroke across the edge. The scrap piece will chip out, but that's what it's there for.

Squaring an edge

I often use a block plane to quickly square an edge on a workpiece. To keep the plane body perpendicular to the sides of the workpiece, I wrap my fingers around the plane (*bottom photo*). Pressing my fingers gently into the side of the workpiece lets me steady the plane and make a clean cut.

Built-in fence

If you're fortunate enough to own a block plane that has an attachable fence (like the Lie-Nielsen skew plane in the top photo), you'll find this feature extremely handy. The fence is a lot more accurate than the finger support method described on the previous page and is adjustable, too. This lets you fine-tune its position for maximum support.

Trimming small pieces

I also regularly use my block plane to fine-tune small parts. This is one of my favorite tools for taking off just a sliver or two of a shaving so that a part fits perfectly.

When I need to take just a bit off the end grain of a small piece, such as when fine-tuning a mitered piece (*middle photo*), I hold the block plane firmly in one hand and pass the workpiece over the blade with the other. It's surprising how much control you have this way, especially if you tuck your elbows into the side of your body. Lock the elbow that's holding the plane and pivot the other with the workpiece. Take light cuts and check the fit often.

Another way to trim small parts—and this is especially useful when you need to take just a bit off the length—is to clamp the plane upside down in your workbench and then pass the workpiece over the blade (*bottom photo*). Take care to keep your fingertips away from the blade; it can't differentiate between wood and flesh.

SHOOTING BOARDS

■ Even in the hands of a master, planing a perfectly square edge on the end of a board is a challenge. That's because the surface of the workpiece itself is used as the reference for square, and odds are that it isn't. That's where a shooting board can come to the rescue. They've been used to square up workpieces for just about as long as there have been planes. A shooting board is a shop-made jig that lets you hold the work square so that you can accurately trim it with a plane. A shooting board can be made to handle 90-degree stock (*top drawing*) or 45-degree miters (*bottom drawing*)—or anything in between, for that matter, since you make it yourself.

Basically, the shooting board is a two-step base made of flat stock with a groove in the bottom piece. The groove collects dust and chips so they don't interfere with the cut. The top step holds one or more cleats that are secured with glue and screws at the desired

angle. The workpiece is held against the cleat, and the plane is laid on its side and passed back and forth over the end of the workpiece to trim it to size.

For all this to work, the sides of the plane chosen must be exactly perpendicular to the sole. To use the shooting board, set the plane for a very fine cut and take several light passes. ShopTip: To help prevent the workpiece from creeping during the cut, glue pieces of sandpaper to the sides of the cleat—they'll grip the workpiece better and hold it in place.

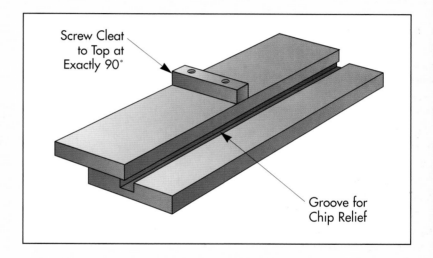

Screw Cleat to Top at Exactly 90°

Groove for Chip Relief

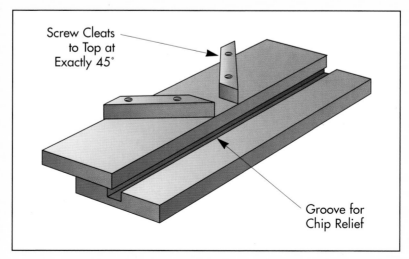

Screw Cleats to Top at Exactly 45°

Groove for Chip Relief

PREMIER TOOL MANUFACTURERS

In addition to the respected tool manufacturers like Stanley, Record, and Starrett, there are a couple of smaller toolmakers that produce tools of exceptional quailty: Bridge City Tool Works and Lie-Nielsen Toolworks. Both of the these companies manufacture what I consider to be premium tools in small batches under tight tolerances, using the finest of materials. By simply picking up one of these fine tools, you'll immediately notice a difference in heft, balance, and finish—the tool fits well in your hand, and the finish is extraordinary.

Bridge City Tool Works

When it comes to tools for layout and measuring, those manufactured by Bridge City Tool Works (www.bridgecitytools.com) have no peers. Bridge City uses the finest materials: brass, rosewood, hardened steel, and their own unique manmade Juara wood (*top photo*). Founded in 1983 by John Economaki, Bridge City Tool Works manufactures tools that are extremely accurate. They are so confident of their accuracy and quality that they offer a lifetime $5.00 guarantee: "For as long as you own a Bridge City Tool Works tool, you may get it recalibrated, resquared or replaced if necessary for five dollars per tool."

Lie-Neilsen Toolworks

If you're looking for the ultimate tools for planing and scraping,

look no further than Lie-Nielsen Toolworks (www.lie-nielsen.com). The hand planes, scrapers, and saws that Tom Lie-Nielsen manufactures in his Warren, Maine, factory are simply a joy to use (*bottom photo*). Just like Bridge City, Lie-Nielsen uses the finest materials, such as manganese bronze for many of his castings and thick Rockwell 60-62 high-carbon tool steel for his blades. Yes, they're expensive, but well worth it.

EDGING TOOLS

There are several specialized edging tools designed with one purpose: to create a rounded or chamfered edge on a workpiece. Three of the more common are the Radi plane, the cornering tool, and the chamfer plane.

Radi plane

Radi planes are wood-bodied planes that hold two concave cutters ground to plane a $1/8$" radius (*top photo*). The cutters can be adjusted up or down independently as desired. The first cutter shears off the majority of the waste, and the second cutter makes a cleanup pass—this lets you make the completed profile in a single pass.

Cornering tool

A cornering tool is a piece of bent steel with notches cut into both ends. These notches are sharpened to create a fixed radius used to accurately round-over an edge (*middle photo*). Common radii are $1/16$", $1/8$", $3/16$", and $1/4$". You position the tool with the notch straddling the edge and then pivot it up until the cutting edge engages the wood. Pulling the tool creates a nice shaving. As always, several light cuts produce a smoother surface than a single deep cut.

Chamfer plane

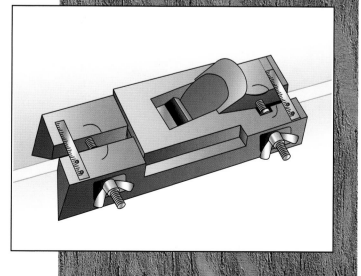

If you regularly plane a lot of chamfers, you might want to consider a chamfer plane (*bottom drawing*). Most of these planes can be adjusted to cut 30-, 45-, and 60-degree chamfers. They work great and will produce a clean, crisp edge without the howling and mess of a portable router.

NOTE: Even though the edging tools mentioned here work fine, I've always felt that a well-tuned block plane can get the job done almost as quickly. However, if you're fighting the clock or are involved with production runs, these specialized tools may be right for you.

Rabbet Planes

The rabbet plane (often called a fillister plane) is used to cut rabbets on the edge of a workpiece, either with or against the grain (*top photos*). Since it is designed specifically for this task, it does an admirable job. The cutter extends the full width of the sole to cut cleanly into corners. A couple of add-on accessories make cutting highly accurate, and repeatable rabbets a breeze. First, there's a guide fence that adjusts in and out on either one or two arm rods that thread into the sole of the plane. Moving the guide in or out sets the width of the rabbet (*bottom drawing*). An adjustable depth gauge on the opposite side lets you set the depth of the rabbet. A three-pointed spur scribes a line in advance of the cutter to help create clean cuts across the grain.

Above photos courtesy of American Tool Companies, Inc., copyright 2001

Two blade positions

I'll never forget when I bought my first used rabbet plane at an auction: a rather nice Stanley No. 78. Since I didn't know much about rabbet planes at the time, I thought it was missing a cutter, as the plane obviously has positions to mount two blades. So I embarrassed myself by asking the auctioneer if he knew where I could pick up a spare blade. He was kind enough to explain that a rabbet plane came with only one blade—the single blade was used in the center position for general rabbet work, and then moved forward to rabbet into a corner (similar to a bull-nose plane; *see pages 87 and 88*). To adjust the depth of cut on a rabbet plane, loosen the knob on the lever cap slightly and then pivot the depth-adjustment lever up and down. When the desired depth is reached, simply tighten the knob.

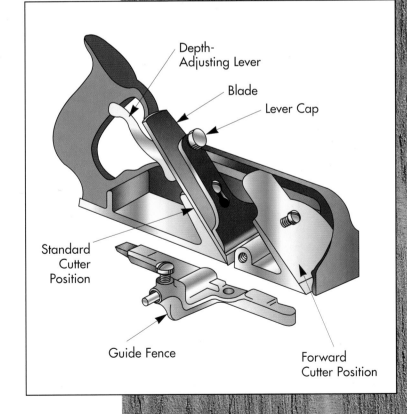

Depth-Adjusting Lever

Blade

Lever Cap

Standard Cutter Position

Guide Fence

Forward Cutter Position

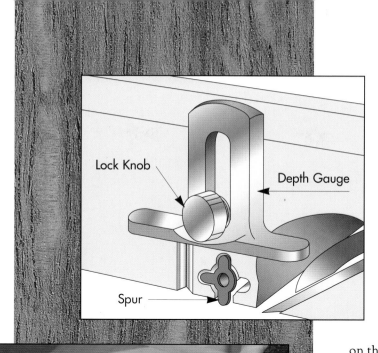

Lock Knob

Depth Gauge

Spur

The spur

Undaunted by my embarrassing question about the missing blade, I asked the auctioneer if he knew where I could buy a replacement spur. The one on my rabbet plane looked like one of its four spurs had broken off. He gently pointed out that it should have only three cutting spurs. The "missing" spur is used for the "idle" position (*top drawing*); that is, it is rotated out of the way when it's not needed—like after you've started a rabbet that's cut with the grain. If you leave the spur down so it's scribing a line continuously, it'll quickly dull. The idle position was created so you could keep the spur on the plane even when it wasn't being used. The logic here was, there was less chance to lose this little beast if you didn't take it off the plane and set it aside, where it would likely get swept away with a pile of shavings and discarded.

Basic use

To use a rabbet plane, start by securing the workpiece to your bench. Then set the guide fence and depth gauge for the desired cut. Make sure the cutting spur is in the active position, and then start the rabbet at the end of the workpiece (*middle photo*). Take a series of light cuts until the shoulder is defined, then slowly work your way backwards to the opposite end (*bottom photo*). If you're planing with the grain, rotate the spur to the idle position once the shoulder is defined. For cross-grain work, leave the spur active the entire time. Take full-length, light strokes; if the blade is sharp, you'll peel off full-length, crispy shavings.

SHOULDER PLANES

After a good jack plane and a low-angle block plane, the next plane I'd suggest a beginning woodworker purchase is a quality shoulder plane (*top photo*). Shoulder planes excel at trimming and fine-tuning joints. They're great for trimming rabbets, shoulders, tenons, dadoes, and grooves. This is the tool to reach for when a joint just doesn't fit right and needs a "tweak" or two to get that perfect fit. Most shoulder planes are all-metal to help create a heavy, dense tool that can effectively prevent or dampen blade chatter. The blade on a shoulder plane runs the full width of the body, and the sides and sole of the plane are ground at perfect right angles to each other (*bottom drawing*).

Shoulder planes come in widths ranging from ½" to slightly over an inch. As on a block plane, the blade is mounted bevel-up and generally has an effective cutting angle of around 37 degrees. This makes it quite good at trimming end grain. Another thing that helps with trimming end grain and making fine cuts in general is an adjustable throat.

On some planes this is adjustable by way of a screw; other planes require that you add or remove shims between the two halves of the body to vary the opening. The blade can be held in place a number of ways. On some larger planes, the blade is often held fast by a lever cap and a locking screw, while others use a more traditional lever cap screw that requires a screwdriver. Smaller shoulder planes generally use a wedge and are adjusted like any wood-bodied plane: You tap on the front or rear of the body to lower or raise the blade.

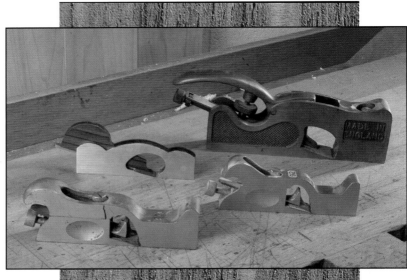

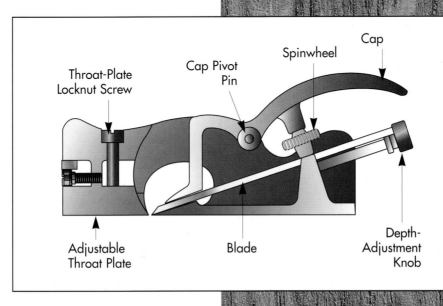

Throat-Plate Locknut Screw

Cap Pivot Pin

Spinwheel

Cap

Adjustable Throat Plate

Blade

Depth-Adjustment Knob

Trimming tenons

My general rule of thumb for cutting mortise-and-tenon joints is to cut the mortise first and then cut the tenons to fit. If you're chopping the mortises by hand (*see pages* 118–120), you'll likely find some variations from mortise to mortise. This means you'll have to trim or fine-tune each tenon to fit: a perfect job for the shoulder plane (*top photo*). Whenever possible, select a plane that's slightly wider than the area you're intending to trim. Make sure to set the plane for a very fine cut and use a razor-sharp blade. As always, take light cuts and make sure to back up the shoulder with a scrap to prevent tear-out.

Smoothing rabbets

Smoothing rabbets is another easy task for a shoulder plane. Position the plane so the side of it butts firmly against the shoulder of the rabbet (*middle photo*). Use as long a shoulder plane as possible, as this helps flatten out any high spots that a shorter-bodied plane might ride up and over. Just as with a tenon, it's important to back up the trailing edge of the rabbet with a scrap to prevent tear-out.

COMBINATION SHOULDER PLANES

There's a nifty type of shoulder plane available that's commonly called a combination plane (*photo at right*). It's basically two planes in one: a shoulder plane and either a bull-nose plane (*see page* 88) or a chisel plane (*see page* 89). The conversion from one to the other is made possible either by lifting off a top piece (*as shown here*) or by removing a front section of the plane. Sometimes this type of plane is called a 3-in-1 plane because it can function as a shoulder plane, bull-nose plane, or chisel plane.

Cutting a rabbet

You'll occasionally hear a shoulder plane referred to as a rabbet plane. That's because it can be used very effectively for this task (*top photo*). The disadvantage to using a shoulder plane versus a rabbet plane is that the shoulder plane doesn't have a built-in guide fence or depth gauge. But one will work in a pinch as long as you clamp a scrap block to the workpiece to guide the cut, and check the depth often with a rule. Also, since a shoulder plane doesn't have cutting spurs, it's a good idea to scribe a starting line when planing cross grain.

Cleaning out a dado

Another job I often assign to a shoulder plane is cleaning out grooves or dadoes. Naturally, it's best to use a shoulder plane that matches the width of the groove or dado, but you can usually get along just fine with a narrower one as long as you check the bottom for flatness often. Keep the side of the plane pressed firmly against the shoulders of the groove or dado as you plane (*middle photo*).

BULL-NOSE PLANES

A bull-nose plane is a special type of shoulder plane that has a very short nose (*photo at right*). Instead of a longer front section, the nose is often only ¼" wide. This makes the plane perfect for delicate work and for reaching in close to corners. The disadvantage to using a bull-nose plane: The short nose allows the plane to travel up and down over undulations instead of flattening them. If you find this happening, it's best to switch to a longer, standard shoulder plane.

CHISEL PLANES

A chisel plane is easily identi-fied by the absence of a fore sole (*top photo*). The advantage to this is that it lets you reach all the way into a corner—when cleaning up a rabbet, for example (*middle drawing*). A chisel plane is also useful for removing glue squeeze-out and for trimming plugs or pegs flush with a surface. The disadvantage to not having a fore sole is that the blade has a ten-dency to vibrate or chatter (*bottom drawing*). This makes the chisel plane generally unfit for regular planing tasks.

A chisel plane in the workshop is like a 1-iron in your golf bag: You won't use it most days, but when the conditions are right, it's the perfect tool for the job. Yes, you could do most of the tasks listed above with other tools; but if your budget permits, you'll be glad you picked up one of these fine tools.

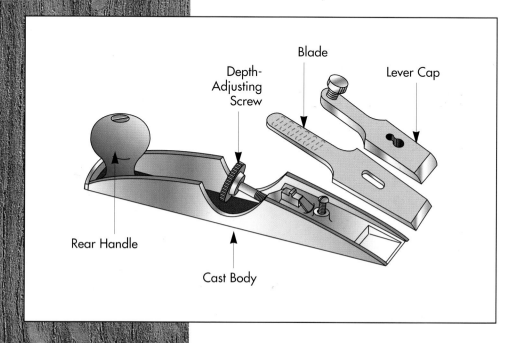

Blade

Depth-
Adjusting
Screw

Lever Cap

Rear Handle

Cast Body

CIRCULAR PLANES

A circular plane (or compass plane, as it's often called) is another one of those specialized planes that'll you'll be glad you have when a project calls for planing a fair curve (*top photo*). The most distinctive feature of a circular plane is that it has a thin, flexible sole (*bottom drawing*). Adjusting the curvature nut forces the sole into either a convex or concave shape. The blade and cap iron rest on a frog that works much like that of any other metal-bodied plane.

Although Record still produces the No. 020C shown here, you can occasionally find a Stanley No. 13 (highly prized by tool collectors) at a tool auction or on the Internet. I realize that many woodworkers would simply grab a belt sander or other electric sanding device to smooth a gradual curve; but a circular plane will leave a cleaner, more fair curve than you can achieve with one of those noisy, dusty tools.

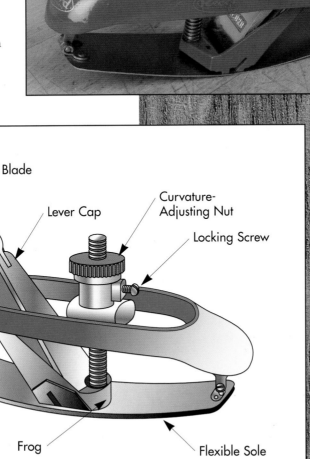

Lateral Adjustment

Blade

Lever Cap

Curvature-Adjusting Nut

Locking Screw

Depth Adjustment

Frog

Flexible Sole

Convex planing

One of the classic uses for a circular plane is truing up the perimeter of a round workpiece, such as a table top (*top photo*). The beauty of using one of these planes is that when the circle is true, you'll know it: The plane's cutting action will slow significantly. To use a circular plane for this, start by adjusting the sole to closely approximate the curve of the workpiece. Adjust the plane blade for a fine cut and start planing. As with any plane, you'll need to be careful to plane with the grain, and not against it. This takes a bit more thought, since the grain direction will change periodically as you work around the top's circumference.

Concave planing

A circular plane also makes quick work of truing up an inside curve (*middle photo*). Though you can start as you did with a convex cut by adjusting the plane's sole to match the inside curve, I've found that if you adjust it so that it's a hair tighter than the inside curve, you'll have better luck. A tighter curve on the sole allows the plane to fit tighter to the curve and makes it easier to lop off the high spots. Once the high spots are gone, you can re-adjust the plane's sole to better match the inside curve. As with a convex cut, it's important to take extra care to prevent planing against the grain (*bottom drawing*). This is one plane that will gladly bury its blade in end grain and tear out a big chunk of wood.

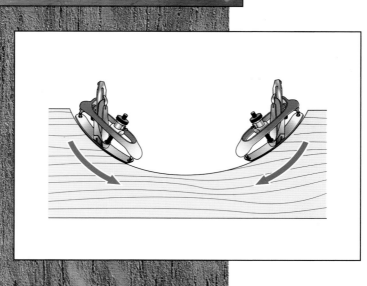

Japanese Planes

I'll admit that I was quite excited to try out my first Japanese plane (*top photo*). Since I had quickly grown so fond of Japanese saws, I thought the planes were sure to find a treasured spot in my tool chest. Although these planes can be very sweet when tuned properly, they do require a substantial amount of fiddling just to get them to work properly. As with any wood-bodied plane, they also require constant attention to make sure they're cutting true. The wood sole can twist or warp and will need to be periodically trued.

Don't get me wrong, I have quite a few wood-bodied planes in my shop; I just don't use them all the time. If I'm in a hurry, I'll stick with a metal-bodied plane that I know will be relatively square and able to get to work right off the shelf. If you don't mind tinkering a bit, you may enjoy a Japanese plane. They do take some getting used to—unlike their Western cousins, Japanese planes cut on the pull stroke.

The body (or dia) of the plane serves as its handles. You wrap your hands, or hand, carefully around the body and pull to create a nice, thin shaving. The simplicity of a Japanese plane (*bottom drawing*) is also one of its primary drawbacks. The laminated blade fits into tapered grooves in the dia, and the chip breaker is held in place by a metal pin. The absence of a frog means you'll have to devote time whenever you use it to properly adjust the blade to the desired depth of cut.

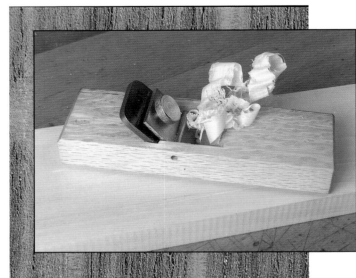

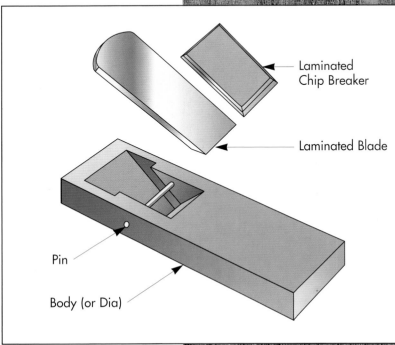

Laminated Chip Breaker

Laminated Blade

Pin

Body (or Dia)

Scrub Planes

A scrub plane (also known as a roughing plane) is another one of those planes that you don't see around the shop very much anymore (*top photo*). That's because they're designed to quickly remove a lot of wood—when thicknessing a board, for example—and this job has been taken over by the electric thickness-planer. In many cases, scrub planes were made from old, worn-out jack planes. The throat was widened to prevent jams, as the shavings were thick and rough. The blade was usually a single cutter with no cap iron (*bottom drawing*).

Curved profile

What makes a scrub plane cut so aggressively is the curved or "scoop" profile ground on its business end (*middle drawing*). A curved grind like this lets you quickly remove a lot of wood. What it doesn't do is leave a smooth surface. But that's irrelevant here; all that a scrub plane is supposed to do is allow you to level a surface quickly, and it does just that.

Convex Blade Profile
Removes Wood Quickly

Basic use

Unlike most traditional planing, a scrub plane can be effectively used against the grain, or more commonly at a 45-degree angle. In addition to leveling surfaces, a scrub plane can also be pressed into service whenever you need to remove a lot of wood fast. The beginning cuts for scooping out a seat, a taper at the end of a workpiece, or even the beginning stages of coopering a door are all tasks that a scrub plane can handle. You can often pick one of these up at an auction or yard sale for a few dollars, or you can make your own by converting an old jack plane.

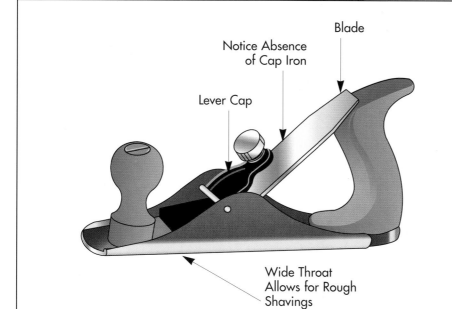

Blade

Notice Absence
of Cap Iron

Lever Cap

Wide Throat
Allows for Rough
Shavings

Combination Planes

Unlike most planes that handle a single task, combination planes (often called multi-planes) were designed to take on many planing jobs. In fact, some manufacturers referred to these planes as "universal" planes. An old Stanley catalog I own (copyright 1909) touts their model No. 55 as a plane that "will do a greater variety of work than can be done with a full line of so called Fancy Planes." Two of the more famous combination planes are the Stanley No. 45 (*top photo*) and No. 55 (*bottom photo*). They can be used to cut grooves, dadoes, rabbets, beads, tongues, ovolos, molding, reeds, hollows and rounds, and nosings. Both consist of a cast-iron body with a wood handle. A fence attaches to the body with a pair of guide rails, and built-in depth adjustment allows for accurate repeat cuts.

Although I'm sure these planes sounded like a great idea to many craftsmen who were tired of lugging around a box of planes, there are a couple of disadvantages to a "universal" plane. First, these beasts require some serious setup time. Every time you want to switch functions, you have to change cutters, add or remove parts, and make some adjustments—not as convenient as reaching into the toolbox for a molding plane. Second, no chip breakers are used and the cutters aren't supported well. Combine these and you have a tendency toward chatter. When the electric router was introduced, combination planes fell by the wayside. Nowadays, they're sought after mostly by tool collectors and individuals who like working wood the old ways. Combination planes are popular with tool restorers because they leave the appropriate tool marks that a router or shaper doesn't.

SCRAPER PLANES

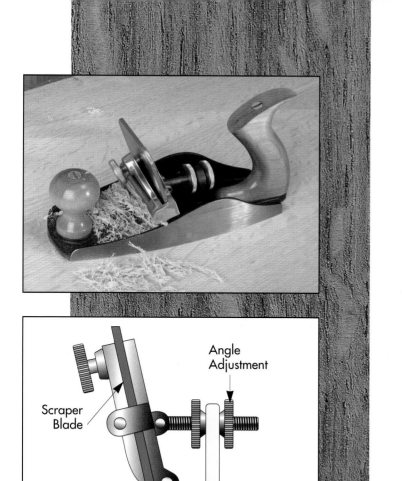

Two of the most often-confused hand tools are the scraper plane and the cabinet scraper (*page* 99). Part of this is because Stanley manufactured a No. 12 scraper plane for many years that somewhat resembles the typical cabinet scraper. There are a number of things, though, that set these two tools apart. A scraper plane (*top photo*) consists of a plane-like body that holds a scraper blade at a precise angle: typically 25 degrees from vertical (*middle drawing*). This makes it the tool of choice for dealing with squirrelly and other hard-to-plane grain.

The big advantage this setup has over the cabinet scraper is that the longer sole prevents it from dipping in and out of surface imperfections; instead, it quickly levels off the surface. And unlike a cabinet scraper, where the scraper blade is bowed (via a thumbscrew) to produce more of a scooping cut, the blade of a scraper plane is flat and cuts along its full width (*bottom drawing*). The blade, however, is sharpened much like that of a cabinet scraper: It's ground to around a 45-degree bevel and then a burr is burnished on the edge (*see pages 186–187 for more on this*).

Angle Adjustment

Scraper Blade

Burr

45° Bevel

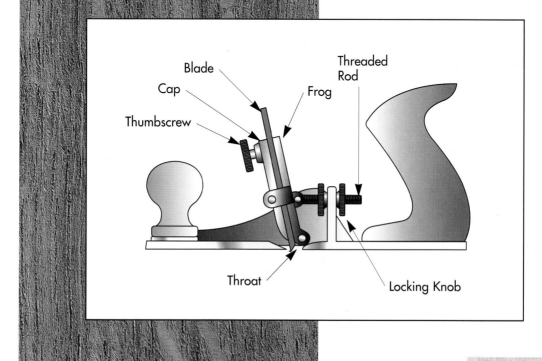

Blade

Cap

Thumbscrew

Frog

Threaded Rod

Throat

Locking Knob

HAND SCRAPERS

The first time I saw a scraper in action, I was sure some form of magic was involved. A cabinet-maker friend of mine was using one to smooth a panel made up of several pieces of tiger-stripe maple. Now this stuff has a deservedly nasty reputation for tearing out while planing. But my friend was pulling off delightfully thin shavings with a hand scraper. It just didn't seem possible to do this with a plain piece of metal about the size of a standard index card (*top photo*).

The scraper wasn't actually plain—its edges had been carefully sharpened and then burnished to form a tiny hook or burr on the end. This burr (*middle drawing*) is what makes a scraper work. In effect, it serves as a tiny plane blade. One of the reasons it works so well on hard-to-plane woods is that the burr is so small. The tight radius of the curve acts as a chip breaker to almost instantly break a shaving so that the chance of tear-out is greatly reduced. The hand scraper is traditionally sharpened at 90 degrees, but some woodworkers prefer the more aggressive 45-degree angle that's common on cabinet scrapers and scraper planes.

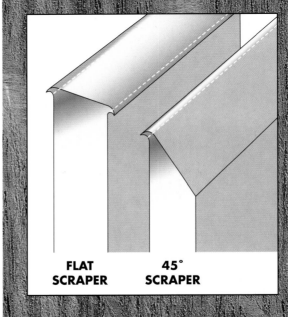

FLAT SCRAPER   **45° SCRAPER**

GOOSENECK SCRAPERS

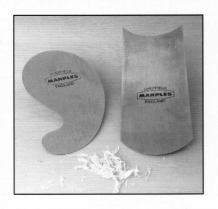

Gooseneck or curved scrapers are a special type of hand scraper designed to let you smooth curved surfaces (*photo at left*). The curves vary along the perimeter so that you can position the scraper to match the curve of your workpiece. These work reasonably well but can be difficult to both sharpen and burnish. As a general rule, I recommend that you find the curve you want, mark a couple of pencil lines on the scraper, and concentrate on sharpening and burnishing just this area. If you were to create a burr along the entire perimeter, it would dig into your fingers during use.

Besides knowing how to sharpen a scraper (*see pages* 186–187), there are a couple of tricks to the "magic" of using a scraper: flexing, finding the angle, and skewing.

Flexing

Technically, you can use a scraper without flexing it at all. The problem is, you're asking the scraper to take off a shaving its full width. For a standard scraper, that's around 4½" to 6" wide! Even with a sharp scraper and a lot of elbow grease this would be difficult. Instead, you can reduce the cutting area by flexing the scraper slightly (*top photo*). Grip the ends of the scraper with both hands, and press lightly in the middle with both thumbs. Note that the greater the flex, the smaller the cutting area and the more of a scooping cut you'll make.

Finding the angle

Here's the tricky part that confuses a lot of woodworkers: finding the correct scraping angle. What makes this such a challenge is that it's different for every scraper, and will most likely change every time you burnish the edge. And that's normal. Burnishing isn't an exact science, and the angle will change. As long as you can feel a burr, all you have to do is tilt the scraper forward or backward until it "bites" into the wood (*middle photo*). When it does, just lock your wrists in this position and start scraping.

Skewing

Just as with a hand plane, skewing a scraper produces more of a shearing cut and will likely produce nicer shavings (*bottom photo*). Note that if you're producing dust, either your scraper is dull or you're at the wrong angle. It's also important to remember that when you skew something, you effectively reduce its ability to smooth out highs and lows—instead, the tool will follow surface undulations.

One of the great scraper debates is whether 'tis nobler to pull or push. I actually use both motions, and in my mind there is no right or wrong way—just go with what feels natural for you.

Pushing

When I've got a lot a scraping to do, I prefer to push the scraper (*top photo*). This method gets more of your body behind the stroke and tends to be less fatiguing overall. I've also found it's easier to maintain the desired flex while pushing, especially if it's flexed a lot and I'm making more of a scooping cut. The disadvantage to pushing is that it lacks the control that pulling a scraper offers.

Pulling

Those who pull a scraper feel it offers better control. I couldn't agree more. Whenever I'm making the finishing passes with a hand scraper, I often switch to the pull stroke (*middle photo*). Among other things, this method lets you see what you're doing—unlike a scraper being pushed, which obscures the surface. The only problem is, I don't find the hand position very comfortable. Instead of my arms being tucked in, they extend away from my body. And flexing the blade soon becomes tiring. It's easy to see why I use this for finish passes and not for the bulk of the removal.

On edge

Occasionally, you may find it useful to use a scraper on edge, such as when you're cleaning out a rabbet (*bottom photo*). Holding it on end allows you to flex the scraper more easily than if it were on its side. However, you'll need to sharpen the end, which will make it uncomfortable to use on its side. I have an old scraper sharpened just for this use.

CABINET SCRAPER

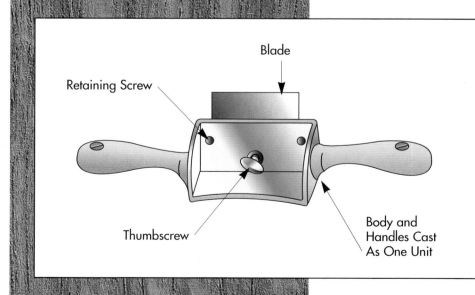

As I mentioned on page 95, the cabinet scraper has often been confused with the scraper plane. The cabinet scraper (often called a double-handled scraper) is designed to reduce the fatigue often associated with hand scraping (*top photo*). It's basically a metal body that holds the scraper blade at a preset angle, typically around 110 degrees. The blade is held in place by a pair of retaining screws, either slotted or with knurled ends (*middle drawing*). The traditional grinding angle of a cabinet scraper's blade is 45 degrees. This creates a sturdy burr that can take a more aggressive cut.

Just like a hand scraper, the blade of a cabinet scraper should be flexed to create the desired depth of cut—and here's where the real beauty of this tool shows. Instead of wearing out your thumbs from flexing, the blade is flexed by way of a thumbscrew that's threaded through the body (*bottom drawing*). To adjust the flex, tighten the retaining screws with the adjustment screw slack. Then tighten the thumbscrew for the desired cut and make a test shaving. Like the scraper plane, a cabinet scraper works well on thin or delicate stock that could easily tear if a hand scraper were to catch or dig into the surface.

Retaining
Screw

Thumbscrew
Adjusts Flex

Blade

CROSS SECTION

Blade

Retaining Screw

Thumbscrew

Body and
Handles Cast
As One Unit

HANDLED SCRAPERS

A variation of the cabinet scraper is the handled scraper (*top photo*). These are designed to be used with either one hand or two. The handled scrapers at left in the photo are called shave hooks, and are basically scraper blades attached to metal rods inserted into wood handles. The scraper blades come in a variety of shapes and sizes and are intended mostly to remove paint and old finishes from moldings and other curved surfaces. But I've found that if you sharpen them properly and roll a nice burr on the end, they can work much better than a gooseneck scraper.

The middle and far right scraper in the top photo are basically paint scrapers, good primarily for removing glue squeeze-out. The Sandvik scraper (*far right in top photo*) features a triangular carbide blade that stands up very well and can be rotated to a fresh edge when one side dulls.

One of my favorite handled scrapers is my grandfather's Stanley No. 82, shown in the middle photo. It's quite an interesting tool that works surprisingly well. Although the actual scraper blade is pretty small, it fits in a sturdy head that can be adjusted to the desired angle. In use, you grip the long handle with one hand and then press down on the front knob with the other (*bottom photo*). This produces a considerable amount of pressure on the blade, and you can remove a lot of wood quickly. At the same time, a light touch can produce thin, wispy shavings. Even though these scrapers aren't being made anymore, you can regularly find them at auctions, at yards sales, and on the Internet for just a couple of dollars.

BEADING TOOLS

A beading tool is sort of a hybrid between a scraper and a plane (*foreground in top photo*). They're often confused with beading planes (*background in top photo*), like my Stanley No. 50, that have molded cutters sharpened like plane blades. To make things even more confusing, this particular beading tool looks a lot like a spokeshave (*see page* 124). A beading tool is designed to hold a variety of cutters to create beads, reeds, flutes, grooves, and other decorative edges. Since they're slow-cutting and work well only with the grain, these have been superseded by the portable router. So it might surprise you to learn that they are still being made. The beading tool shown here is made by Lie-Nielsen Toolworks (www.lie-nielsen.com) and is a reproduction of the old Stanley No. 66.

So if the beading tool has been replaced by the router, why is it still being made? Nostalgia? The answer is that this classic tool still outperforms its modern counterpart in two important ways. First, the small "sole" of the tool allows you to easily follow a three-dimensional curve (such as a cabriole leg), where the larger base of a router can't travel. Second, you can make your own cutters to match antique molding—or create your own, for that matter.

A beading tool is similar to a cabinet scraper in that the cutter rests against the body at a preset angle and is held in place with one or more retaining screws (*bottom drawing*). Quality beading tools come with one or more fences that help guide the cutter along the edge of the workpiece.

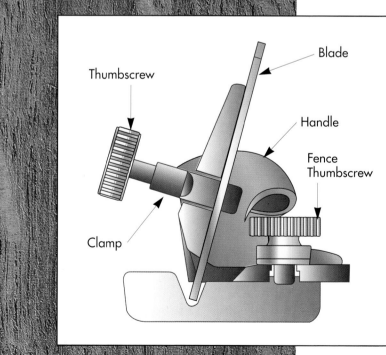

Thumbscrew

Blade

Handle

Fence Thumbscrew

Clamp

Selecting the cutter

To use a beading tool, start by selecting the desired cutter. Loosen the knurled knob and slide the cutter in place (*top photo*). If you can't find the profile you're looking for, Lie-Nielsen supplies blanks with the tool so you can grind any profile you want (technically, the negative of the profile you want). Just make sure to flatten the back of the cutter just as you would a plane blade, and then sharpen the profile with slip-stones or diamond hones.

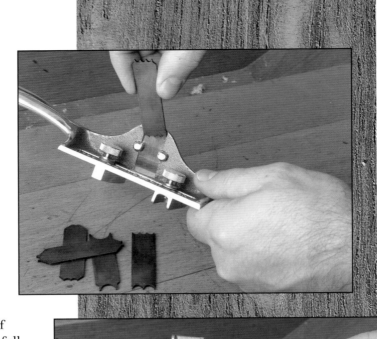

Adjusting the cutter

Once you've got the cutter installed, you can adjust it (*middle photo*). If the cutter is small, you can adjust it for a full cut from the start. For larger cutters, I recommend setting it so just the first $1/16$" or so protrudes, and then make a few passes. Then lower the cutter an additional $1/16$" and repeat until the full profile is reached. You'll also want to adjust the fence or fences to position the cutter on the workpiece at the correct starting point.

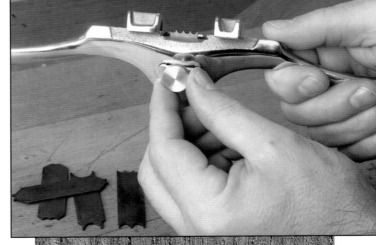

Basic use

The big thing to keep in mind when using a beading tool is patience. Even when sharpened correctly, these tools are very slow-cutting. Relax and take your time. Enjoy watching the profile slowly take shape. For your first couple of passes, take it easy on the downward pressure (*bottom photo*). Let the tool begin the cut. Once it's clearly started, apply gentle pressure and keep the tool moving.

SHOP-MADE SCRATCH STOCK

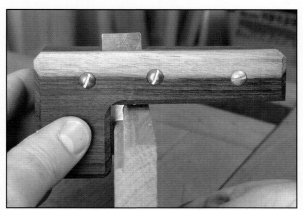

Home-made beading tools or "scratch stocks" could be found in every cabinetmaker's toolbox in the past. Although they took a lot longer to use, they were a lot less expensive than a molding plane, and a new cutter could be made in a short while.

A scratch stock is basically just a handle with a kerf cut in it to accept a cutter. Screws pass through the kerfed portion of the stock to pinch the cutter in place (*bottom drawing*). These are very easy to make and can be a lot of fun to use. NOTE: To hold the cutter as securely as possible, I suggest using machine screws that pass through the body; then thread on nuts.

Making your own cutter

You can make your own cutter from an old scraper blade or broken saw blade. Just draw out the negative of the profile you're after and grind or file away the waste (*top photo*). Make sure to flatten the back of the cutter and hone the edge sharp with slipstones.

Basic use

Since the cutter for a scratch stock is a scraper, you'll have to tilt it to find the correct cutting angle (*middle photo*). Pivot the stock until cutting action begins. Just as with a beading tool, use little downward pressure at first and take light cuts. As the profile begins to take shape, apply gentle pressure and take your time.

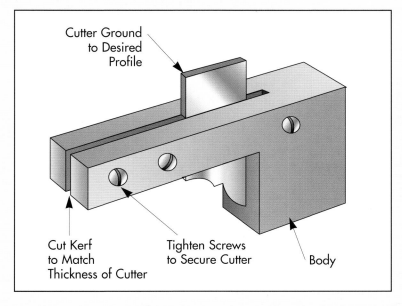

Cutter Ground to Desired Profile

Cut Kerf to Match Thickness of Cutter

Tighten Screws to Secure Cutter

Body

SANDPAPER

No chapter about smoothing tools would be complete without discussing sandpaper. Like many woodworkers, I loathe sanding. It's messy work that I try to keep to a minimum. Whenever possible, I reduce hand- or power-sanding with the appropriate use of planes and scrapers. But unless a project consists mainly of flat, square surfaces (like many Craftsman-style designs), I end up using sandpaper for final smoothing.

Types of sandpaper

There are three main types of sandpaper that are commonly used in a woodshop: silicon-carbide, garnet, and aluminum-oxide (*top to bottom in the top photo*). For years, all that was available was garnet sandpaper, made from finely crushed semiprecious stones. This type of paper tends to dull and wear out quickly but has the best reputation for smoothing without leaving scratches. Silicon-carbide paper (often called wet/dry sandpaper) is used primarily for sanding between coats of finish, since it can be used wet. Aluminum-oxide is a relatively new abrasive that stands up well and lasts much longer than garnet.

Regardless of the type of abrasive, all sandpaper is categorized by grits that define the size of the particle (*see the chart below*).

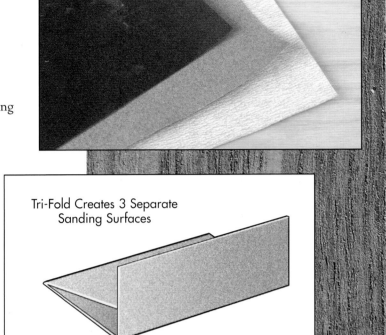

Tri-Fold Creates 3 Separate Sanding Surfaces

SANDPAPER GRITS

Specified grit ANSI* CAMI**	600	400	320	280	240	220	180	150	120	100	80	60
Particle size (in microns)	16	23.6	36	44	53.5	64	79	95	113	136	189	266

*ANSI = American National Standards Institute   **CAMI = Coated Abrasive Manufacturers Institute

Although there are many rules of thumb for grit selection, I've found that I usually need only two for smoothing. I start with 150-grit and then finish with 220. This is possible because I don't expect the sandpaper to do what I should have done with a plane or a scraper. Instead of grinding away at an imperfection with a power sander, I'll remove it first with a plane or scraper. Many woodworkers don't realize that it's actually faster this way.

Hand-sanding

If you're planning on sanding by hand, I suggest ripping a standard 9"×11" sheet in half across its width and then folding it in thirds, as shown in the middle drawing on the opposite page. This creates three separate sanding surfaces that can be folded over in turn to produce a fresh surface as the other two sides wear out. Just as important, folding the paper like this prevents the grit side of sandpaper from rubbing against itself, which will dull it before you even have a chance to use it.

Sanding block

I also strongly recommend a sanding block, especially if you're working on a flat surface. A sanding block helps to distribute sanding pressure evenly and reduces hand fatigue (*bottom photo on opposite page*). Although you can purchase many snazzy sanding blocks with complicated levers and fancy hold-downs, I've always felt a scrap of wood or a cork block wrapped with sandpaper works best. You can quickly change paper and even modify the block to make it better suit the job at hand. As with any sanding, make sure to sand with the grain to prevent cross-grain scratches. Also, clean the sandpaper often by removing it from the sanding block and giving it a sharp rap on the edge of your workbench.

SANDING PLATE

Years ago, the folks at Sandvik came up with a terrific product called a sanding plate that I've grown quite fond of (*photo at right*). It's basically a serrated metal plate that works sort of like a cheese grater for wood. Precision holes are punched in the hardened steel to create tiny, volcano-like craters with sharp edges (*drawing at right*). Since these holes are made with much accuracy, the resulting steel plate performs like varying grades of sandpaper, but it doesn't wear out and it rarely, if ever, clogs. The sanding plate is cut into different shapes and sizes and is attached to plastic handles—some in the form of a sanding block, others like files. When the plate finally does wear out, you can strip it off and slap on a replacement plate.

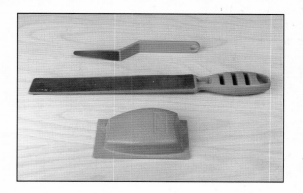

"...I feel I can not too strongly inveigle against carving executed by machinery.... The carving so executed is false in itself; since it is not an original process, but rather one counterfeiting a slow, patient, intelligent operation, whose beautiful results can only be obtained through the sole medium of the human hand...."

GUSTAV STICKLEY (1905)

SHAPING TOOLS

When it's time to fine-tune a joint, that's when you reach for a chisel. To make that smooth round-over on a cabriole leg, only a good file or rasp will do. For that personal touch a machine can't duplicate, like carved detail on a cabinet pull, a gouge is a good choice. All these shaping tools are guided solely by the hand, and that's what makes their effects so personal and unique. Unlike hand planes, which use a sole to guide the cutter, for example, all the direction and control of shaping tools is from the hands. That's what makes them so special: No machine can duplicate their results.

Think of the chamfered ends of Brian Boggs's chairs, or the crisp through tenons of Stickley's work. They quietly declare themselves made by hand...made with care and attention...made by one skilled human being. Anyone can use a sander, and its machine-powered abrasives can obliterate any "mistake." Not everyone has the guts, or the skill, to leave their mark on a piece with a shaping tool. The confidence to do that comes with a little knowledge and a keen edge.

Top left to right: Stanley No. 53 spokeshave; mortise chisel made by Williams, Morse, & Co.; Nicholson USA flat standard file with unmarked cast-iron handle; chisel made by Wm. Taylor, 1½" wide, 15" long; Nicholson "platers special" file, woodworker's slick, made by Underhill Edge Tool Co.; round carving chisel made by W. Butcher; folding-handle drawknife made by J. S. Cantelo, patented December 18, 1833.

CHISEL TERMINOLOGY

Chisels can be broadly classified into two groups: those designed for use with hand pressure only, and those intended to be driven by a mallet. Chisels made for hand use only may be either firmer chisels (originally called "former" chisels because they were used to form rough shapes) or paring chisels. Mallet-driven chisels are mostly thick, stout chisels used to chop mortises. Over time, any heavy-duty chisel became known as a mortise chisel, even though they could be used for carving or other shaping work.

Most chisels are similar in appearance. They each have a wood or plastic handle and a blade with a tang or socket (*bottom drawing*). What sets them apart primarily is the profile of the blade (*top drawing*) and their respective grinds or cutting angles (*middle drawing*).

Mortise chisels are easily identified by their thick, almost square blades. The bevel is ground to a steep angle to hold up under the constant blows of a mallet. Firmer chisels can have either square or beveled edges. The bevel for square-edged firmer chisels is usually a bit steeper than for bevel-edged chisels, which are most often used for paring. Note that in the middle drawing two sets of angles are given. As a general rule of thumb, chisels used on hardwoods require a steeper bevel to cut effectively than those used on softwoods.

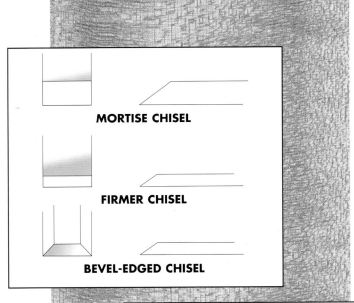

MORTISE CHISEL

FIRMER CHISEL

BEVEL-EDGED CHISEL

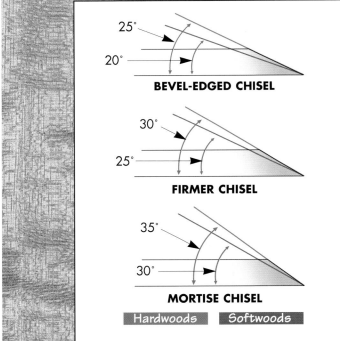

25°
20°
BEVEL-EDGED CHISEL

30°
25°
FIRMER CHISEL

35°
30°
MORTISE CHISEL

Hardwoods   Softwoods

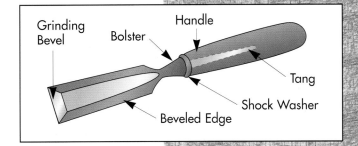

Grinding Bevel
Bolster
Handle
Tang
Shock Washer
Beveled Edge

METAL HARDNESS

One of the most important characteristics of a chisel that affects its ability to hold an edge—and its overall performance—is its hardness. The hardness of metal is tested using two common methods: the Brinell test and the Rockwell test.

The Brinell test

In this test, a hardened steel ball is pressed into the smooth surface of the metal to make an indentation that's measured under a microscope. Once the spherical area of the indentation is calculated (taking into account the pressure applied), the stress per unit of area when the ball comes to rest is calculated, and the hardness number obtained.

The Rockwell test

With the Rockwell test, a metal ball or cone with a known hardness is pressed into the metal being tested. The Rockwell hardness is defined at the point of deformation of, or penetration into, the metal being tested. The Rockwell Scale, developed in conjunction with the ASTM (American Society for Testing and Materials), is the most-often-used measure of metal hardness in the world today. In general,

the higher the alphanumeric designation, the harder the metal. So, a "C" is harder than a "B", a "30" is harder than a "20," etc. The C scale is the most-used Rockwell scale and is often denoted Rc. Chisels made with steel tested at Rc 58 to 62 have been proven over time to stand up well.

METAL HARDNESS

Brinell Hardness tungsten-carbide ball 3000 Kg	Rockwell A scale 60 Kg	Rockwell C scale 150 Kg	Brinell Hardness tungsten-carbide ball 3000 Kg	Rockwell A scale 60 Kg	Rockwell C scale 150 Kg
	85.6	68.0	444	74.2	47.1
	85.3	67.5	429	73.4	45.7
	85.0	67.0	415	72.8	44.5
767	84.7	66.4	401	72.0	43.1
757	84.4	65.9	388	71.4	41.8
745	84.1	65.3	375	70.6	40.4
733	83.8	64.7	363	70.0	39.1
722	83.4	64.0	352	69.3	37.9
712	—	—	341	68.7	36.6
710	83.0	63.3	331	68.1	35.5
698	82.6	62.5	321	67.5	34.3
684	82.2	61.8	311	66.9	33.1
682	82.2	61.7	302	66.3	32.1
670	81.8	61.1	293	65.7	30.9
656	81.3	60.1	285	65.3	29.9
653	81.2	60.0	277	64.6	28.8
647	81.1	59.7	269	64.1	27.9
638	80.8	59.2	262	63.6	26.6
630	80.6	58.8	255	63.0	25.4
627	80.5	58.7	248	62.5	24.2
601	79.8	57.3	241	61.8	22.8
578	79.1	56.0	235	61.4	21.7
555	78.4	54.7	229	60.8	20.5
534	77.8	53.5	223	—	20.0
514	76.9	52.1	217	—	18.0
495	76.3	51.0	212	—	17.0
477	75.6	49.6	207	—	16.0
461	74.9	48.5	201	—	15.0

BEVEL-EDGED CHISELS

When I say "chisel," the image that pops into most woodworkers' minds is a bevel-edged chisel like any of those shown in the top photo. It's ironic that these chisels have been marketed so long as bevel-edged that most people don't realize that these are actually firmer chisels. What's really odd is that many woodworkers think that firmer chisels are a completely different type of chisel. A bevel-edged chisel is just a standard firmer chisel where the edges have been beveled up toward the top of the blade.

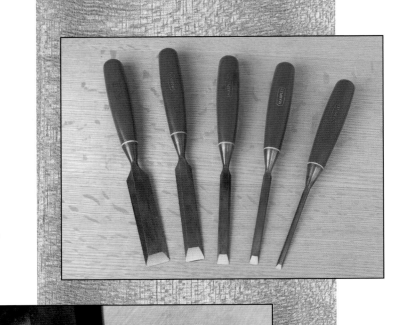

As I mentioned earlier, the advantage to beveling the edges is that this produces a chisel more adept at fitting into tight places, such as when removing the waste or trimming between dovetails (*middle photo*). This same slim profile allows a bevel-edged chisel to trim sliding dovetails (*bottom photo*) and other hard-to-reach places. The downside to beveling the edges is that it removes metal that would normally stiffen the chisel. This makes bevel-edged chisels more suitable for delicate work. I have occasionally taken a mallet to mine, but if I've got a lot of wood to remove, I generally use a square-edged firmer chisel or a mortise chisel. Bevel-edged chisels can be purchased individually or in sets, in widths ranging from 1/8" up to 2". The most common set consists of six chisels: 1/8", 1/4", 3/8", 1/2", 3/4", and 1".

HANDLE VARIATIONS

■ I bought my first set of quality chisels from a mail-order catalog. I picked a set with blades made from Sheffield steel and what looked like comfortable handles. The second I unpacked one and held it in my hand, I knew that it didn't feel right. But being a novice, I figured the manufacturer knew what they were doing and it must be me. So I kept them—and used them for many (uncomfortable) years. What a bonehead!

It wasn't until I was visiting a woodworking buddy that I saw the light. My friend was cutting a set of dovetails in wide planks for a blanket chest he was building for his daughter. I commented on his well-worn chisels, and he handed one to me. I couldn't believe how good it felt in my hand. The balance was near perfect; the handle fit so well in my palm that it felt like an extension of my hand. So this is what a chisel should feel like, I thought.

I decided then and there to always trust my first impression of a tool. I should have sent that first set back and ordered something else. Better yet, I should have visited a woodworking store and tried each brand until I found the best fit. I realize this might sound excessive, but chisels are some of the most-often-used hand tools in any shop. They really should mold to your hand and feel great. Naturally, handle style (*bottom drawing*) and the material used are matters of personal preference.

I have four sets of chisels in my shop: a set of large, stout mortise chisels; a set of Marples plastic-handled (virtually unbreakable) firmer chisels for moderately heavy work; a set of Marples "blue chip" bevel-edged chisels for rough paring and shaping; and an exquisite set of bevel-edged Japanese chisels for all my fine work (fitting joints, cutting dovetails, etc.). I also have a few specialty chisels, but the bulk of the work is done with these four sets.

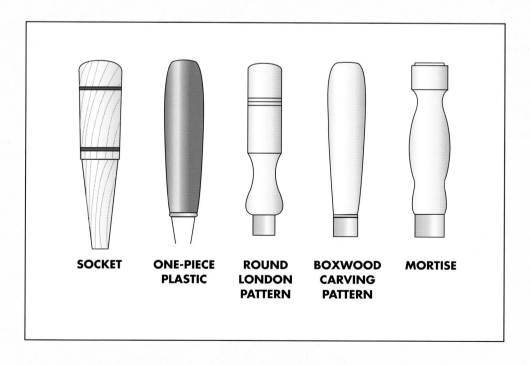

| SOCKET | ONE-PIECE PLASTIC | ROUND LONDON PATTERN | BOXWOOD CARVING PATTERN | MORTISE |

GRIPS

There are three widespread grips used with chisels: underhand, overhand, and the blade grip. Each may be used to cut a single joint.

Underhand grip

I use the underhand grip most often when I'm making a paring cut. With this grip, the handle of the chisel rests in the palm of one hand while the fingers of the other hand guide the blade (*top photo*). As you lean forward, the blade begins to pare. At any point, you can quickly stop the cut by "pinching" the blade with your fingers.

Overhand grip

The overhand grip is especially useful for vertical paring cuts, such as when cleaning out a mortise or trimming the shoulders of a tenon (*middle photo*). One hand wraps around the chisel (typically with the thumb resting on top), and the other hand guides the blade. This grip lets you get your shoulder and weight into the cut and works especially well when trimming stubborn end grain.

Blade grip

Another grip I often use is the blade grip (*bottom photo*). Here, I grip the chisel by only the blade so that I can use my other hand for the mallet to drive the chisel. This grip lets me position the chisel tip with pinpoint accuracy. Another version of the blade grip is the slicing cut, shown in the bottom photo on the opposite page.

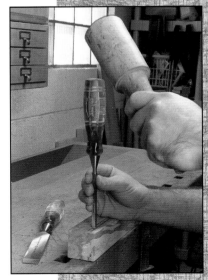

BASIC CHISEL TECHNIQUE

Whatever chisel work you're planning, the first step is to secure the workpiece. For light work, such as paring, you can just clamp the workpiece in your bench vise. But if you're doing heavier work (especially rigorous work like chopping mortises), clamp the workpiece to the top of the bench. For the best support, try to position it directly over (or as close as possible to) the legs of the workbench (*top photo*). This helps dampen vibration and prevents the workpiece from bowing under heavy blows.

Support block

For chisel work where you're paring the full width of the workpiece, or through the workpiece, you should always insert a support block under it (*middle photo*). A support block not only protects your workbench from certain damage, but also helps prevent tear-out by solidly supporting the wood fibers where the chisel exits the work.

Slicing cut

Although I've always considered a slicing cut to be one of the more basic chisel techniques, I rarely see it being used. This specialized form of the blade grip should be in everyone's bag of tricks. I use two forms of this cut. With one, I grip the blade almost like a pencil and use it vertically to lightly pare away wood (*top photo on page 116*). With the other form, I grip the blade with one hand and use the other to form a fulcrum. This way, I can pivot the chisel into the workpiece, such as when slicing a dowel flush with a surface (*bottom photo*). Either way, it's a great grip.

TRIMMING TENONS

A common paring task for a chisel is trimming or cleaning tenons for a mortise-and-tenon, a slip joint, or a stub-tenon-and-groove joint. There are a couple of critical areas of the tenon that usually need attention: the cheeks and the shoulders.

Cheeks

The first thing I do when fitting a mortise-and-tenon joint is to check the fit of the tenon in the mortise. Since it's always better to have a tenon that's too big (if it's too small, you'll need to recut it), the tenon will often require a little paring to fit snugly. I use a wide chisel for this and an underhand grip to lightly pare away the excess (*top photo*). Start at one end and use the lip created by the chisel to reference the next cut. Take light cuts and check the fit often.

Shoulder

Once the tenon fits into the mortise, all that's left is to make sure the joint fits snugly together with no gaps. Even when you're careful cutting a tenon, it's easy to end up with a "stepped" shoulder. To clean up the shoulders, start by taking light, horizontal paring strokes to clean out the intersection of the cheek and shoulder (*middle photo*). A long time ago I learned the value of "undercutting" the shoulders. That is, instead of making a 90-degree cut, I just start inside the shoulder (around $1/16$") and tilt the chisel up slightly (*bottom drawing*). This undercuts the shoulder and virtually eliminates any fitting problems.

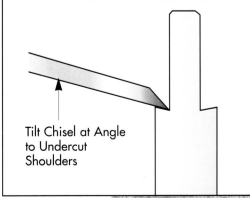

Tilt Chisel at Angle to Undercut Shoulders

CLEANING OUT MORTISES

The other half of a mortise-and-tenon joint, the mortise, often requires some "tweaking" after it has been cut. If I've cut the mortises by hand, I usually only need to tweak the tenons for a good fit. If you use a machine, you may need to do a little or a lot of work. If the mortises are router-cut, they'll likely only need the corners squared. If you drilled them out, you've got considerable work to do.

Sides

To clean up the sides of a mortise, choose a sharp chisel that's fairly wide (*top photo*). Take care to keep the chisel vertical (a guide block clamped to the workpiece helps), and take light cuts. Skewing the chisel also produces a cleaner shearing cut.

Ends

Mortise ends often require paring, either to size the mortise correctly or to square up corners (*middle photo*). Although a lot of folks advise using a chisel that's the same width as the mortise for this, I've had better luck with one that's slightly narrower. This way the chisel doesn't get jammed between the sides, and you don't have to rock it to get it out. Rocking like that can enlarge the mortise, creating a sloppy fit.

Bottom

The bottom of a mortise is a difficult area to clean up, since access is limited by the sides and ends. The best way I've found to do this is to use a chisel with the bevel up and take light, scooping cuts (*bottom photo*). Avoid the temptation of using the top edge of the mortise end as a fulcrum point for the chisel: You'll only crush this edge and end up with a weaker joint.

Trimming Grooves

In addition to cleaning up mortises and tenons, I routinely use a chisel to fine-tune grooves, rabbets, dadoes, and other joints.

Paring sides

One of the more common paring tasks is removing just a bit of material from the side of a groove or other joint. Whenever possible, I use the blade grip for this and take a slicing cut (*top photo*). This offers a couple of advantages over the more conventional vertical paring stroke. First, skewing the blade creates a cleaner shearing cut. Also, it makes it easy to slide the flat back of the chisel along the side of the groove or dado as a steady starting point. This way you start with a very light cut and ease into the waste.

Ends of the groove

Whether a groove is cut by hand or by machine, there's often a tendency for the final few inches of the groove to be the incorrect depth. This can be caused by letting up on the workpiece as it passes over a spinning bit or blade, or by easing pressure near the end of a cut made by hand. To correct the depth, I use an underhand grip and pare away the waste with a series of light cuts (*middle photo*). See page 121 for a handy tip on using a gauge block to gauge the depth accurately.

Cleaning up the bottom

Cleaning up the bottom of a groove is fairly straightforward. Here again, flip the chisel so the bevel is down, and run it along the bottom (*bottom photo*). Inverting the bevel like this prevents it from catching and digging into the groove.

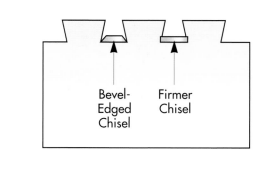
Photo courtesy of American Tool Companies, Inc., copyright 2001

FIRMER CHISELS

Firmer chisels are general-purpose woodworking chisels that are some of the workhorses of any shop (*top photo*). When most woodworkers think of firmer chisels, they envision rather stout, square-sided chisels like those shown in the top photo. But bevel-edged chisels (*see page 110*) are also firmer chisels—their sides are just tapered up toward the top. Most firmer chisels have blades roughly 4" long and come in widths varying from $1/8$" up to 2". The handles may be wood or plastic.

Profile

The basic difference between a firmer chisel and a bevel-edged firmer chisel is its profile (*middle drawing*). The square sides of a firmer chisel create a strong blade that's fully capable of handling light to moderate mallet blows. The advantage of beveling the edges is that it gives greater access when trimming joints such as dovetails. The downside to this: The blade is not as stout as a standard firmer chisel's, and so a mallet should be used sparingly and lightly with this more delicate chisel.

Bevel-
Edged
Chisel

Firmer
Chisel

Anatomy

A firmer chisel consists of three parts: blade, handle, and ferrule. In most cases, the blade has a tang that fits into a hole drilled into the end of the handle (*bottom drawing*). The ferrule (often brass) helps prevent the tang from splitting the handle if the chisel is struck with a mallet. Registered mortise chisels are often confused with firmer chisels because they look alike. This is how you can usually tell the difference: A registered mortise chisel typically has a thicker blade and a ferrule on the end of the handle to prevent "crowning," or mushrooming of the handle end.

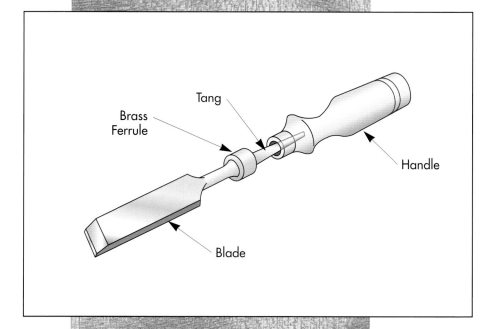

Brass
Ferrule

Tang

Handle

Blade

MORTISE CHISELS

Mortise chisels are distinguished by their thick, beefy blades and stout handles (*top photo*), both designed to handle the heavy mallet blows associated with chopping mortises by hand. But the blades are thicker for another, less obvious reason: The wide blade helps guide the chisel and keep it square to the sides of the mortise as it's being cut. This is a big plus, because it makes the chisel almost self-guiding once the sides and ends of the mortise are established. It's another key reason why this is absolutely the tool of choice for cutting mortises by hand.

Handle options

There are two basic handle options available for mortise chisels: tang-mount and socket-mount (*bottom drawing*). With a tang-mount, the tang on the end of the blade fits into a hole drilled into the end of the handle. Generally, a leather washer is added between the base of the blade and the handle to serve as a shock absorber. On socket-style mortise chisels, a tenon is turned on the end of the handle to fit into the socket on the end of the blade. The disadvantage of a tang-style mortise chisel is that repeated blows will tend to drive the tang deeper into the handle. Even with ferrules installed at both ends of the handle, the tang will eventually make the handle split. This rarely happens with a socket-style chisel.

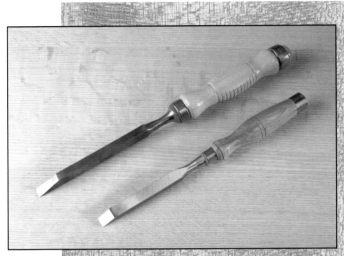

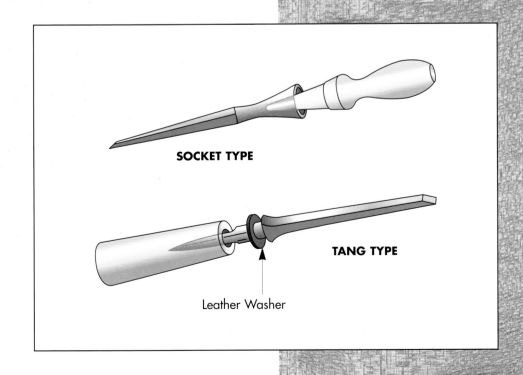

SOCKET TYPE

TANG TYPE

Leather Washer

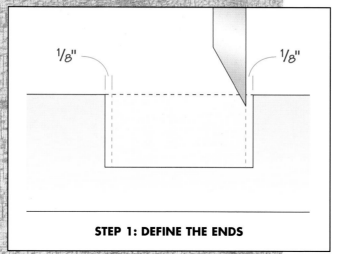

STEP 1: DEFINE THE ENDS

1/8"   1/8"

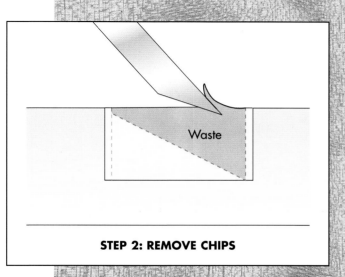

Waste

STEP 2: REMOVE CHIPS

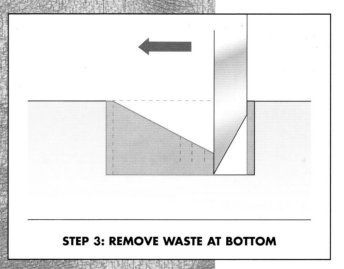

STEP 3: REMOVE WASTE AT BOTTOM

The first time I chopped a mortise by hand, it was a disaster. I used a small, bevel-edged chisel that was relatively dull (I hadn't quite figured out sharpening yet). After half an hour of pounding on that poor board, I had a lopsided hole that looked more like a crater than a mortise. The width varied, the sides were rough, and the bottom was a jumble of torn slivers of wood. I had made three mistakes: I was using an improperly sharpened tool, I was using the wrong tool (I should have used a stout mortise chisel), and I was using the wrong technique.

Decades later, I find chopping a mortise by hand a pleasure—really. Sure, it's a bit physical, but it's very rewarding. I often will hand-chop a mortise if I've got only a few to make. It's actually quicker than going through the whole machine setup and test-cut business.

Define the ends and remove waste

After you've laid out the mortise and clamped the workpiece firmly to your bench (preferably over a leg), start by defining the ends. Position the mortise chisel (the same width as the mortise) so that the flat is toward the end of the mortise about 1/8" from the layout line (I'll explain why later). Then drive the chisel vertically into the mortise about 1/4" with a mallet (*top drawing*). Next, tip the chisel over so the bevel is down, and remove a chip (*middle drawing*). Once you've reached the desired depth of the mortise, start working across, cleaning out the waste at the bottom. Hold the chisel vertically and take light, paring cuts (*bottom drawing*).

Continue removing waste from the bottom, working your way toward the opposite end of the mortise. Take light cuts and pry out the waste with the chisel (*top drawing*). ShopTip: For a simple depth gauge, wrap a piece of tape around the blade of the chisel.

Finish cuts

Once the full width of the mortise is complete, you can make your finish cuts to the ends. By now you've probably figured why it's important to leave 1/8" or so on the ends of the mortises while you chop out the majority of the waste. Even when you're careful prying out the waste, there's a tendency to use the top edge of the mortise as a fulcrum for the blade. The result is that this edge gets crushed. If the mortises are stopped, the tenon will cover this, but the joint won't be as sturdy as it could be. But if the mortise is a through mortise, this will be highly visible. Leaving a bit of waste to be trimmed away as a final step yields clean, crisp edges (*middle drawing*).

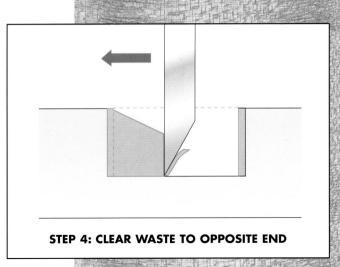

STEP 4: CLEAR WASTE TO OPPOSITE END

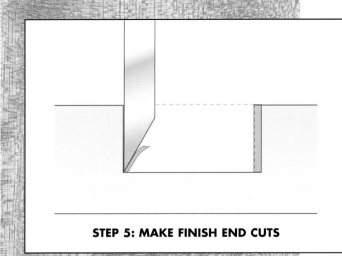

STEP 5: MAKE FINISH END CUTS

TIGHTENING A LOOSE HANDLE

■ Since mortise chisels really do take a beating, the handles can and do come loose occasionally. When this happens, here's an easy way to fix it. Whether the blade fits into the handle with a tang or a socket (as shown here), you can insert a small wood shim or two to take up the slack (*left photo*). Then simply hammer the handle back on. Another method that works well on sockets is to wrap a curled shaving around the "tenon" of the handle before driving the handle back in place.

PARING CHISELS

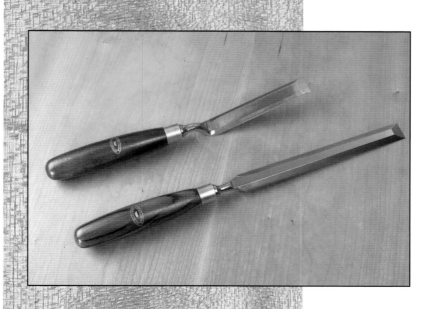

A paring chisel is similar in appearance to a firmer chisel except the blade is much longer (*top photo*). The blade on a firmer chisel is usually around 4" to $4^1/_2$" long, while the average paring chisel blade is 7" to 8" long (*bottom drawing*). This type of chisel was a standard item in a cabinetmaker's tool chest, but it was largely replaced by the electric router.

The long blade of a paring chisel made it perfect for trimming the bottoms of grooves and dadoes cut to accept shelves and other carcass parts. Once the router entered the scene, with its ability to cut perfectly flat-bottomed grooves, the paring chisel began to disappear.

Because the blade of a paring chisel is so long, it's fairly fragile, and a mallet should never be used. Hand pressure is all that's suitable for paring chisels. If you plan to use a paring chisel to flatten the bottom of a groove, consider making a gauge block to accurately hold the blade at the desired height (*middle drawing*). Occasionally, you can find a paring chisel with a "crank" neck where the handle is offset from the blade (*bottom chisel in bottom drawing*). This lets you pare with the blade flat against the workpiece.

Groove

Gauge Block

Handle

Bevel-Edged Blade

SOCKET STYLE

Handle

Brass Ferrule

Firmer Blade

Tang

TANG STYLE

CORNER CHISELS

A corner chisel is a special type that has two cutting edges that meet at a perfect 90-degree angle (*top photo*). NOTE: The chisel shown here is available from Lie-Nielsen Toolworks (www.lie-nielsen.com). Corner chisels are used to square up the corners of a mortise after most of the waste has been removed. Because these chisels are challenging to sharpen, I use mine only for the finish paring cuts. This way, the edge lasts longer than if I used it to remove a lot of waste. Granted, this tool isn't for everyone; but if you do cut a lot of mortises—especially through mortises—you'll really appreciate this tool. Since I build a lot of Craftsman-style furniture with exposed joinery, a corner chisel comes in quite handy.

Two cutting edges

Look closely at the business end of a corner chisel: You'll find flat faces on the exterior of the blade and a notch ground into the inside face to create two cutting edges (*middle photo*). These edges are honed to create both a razor-sharp tool and a sharpening challenge. You can't sharpen this tool with a standard stone; you'll need slipstones or, better yet, small diamond hones. I suggest maintaining the edges by giving each a couple of strokes with a diamond hone before every use.

Basic use

The key to using a corner chisel effectively is to take light, paring cuts and make sure to hold the chisel perfectly vertical (*bottom photo*). I often clamp a square scrap block to the workpiece to help guide the chisel in straight. Stop often and clean out the waste. If you're cutting a through mortise, it's best to cut halfway, flip the workpiece, and continue in from the other side.

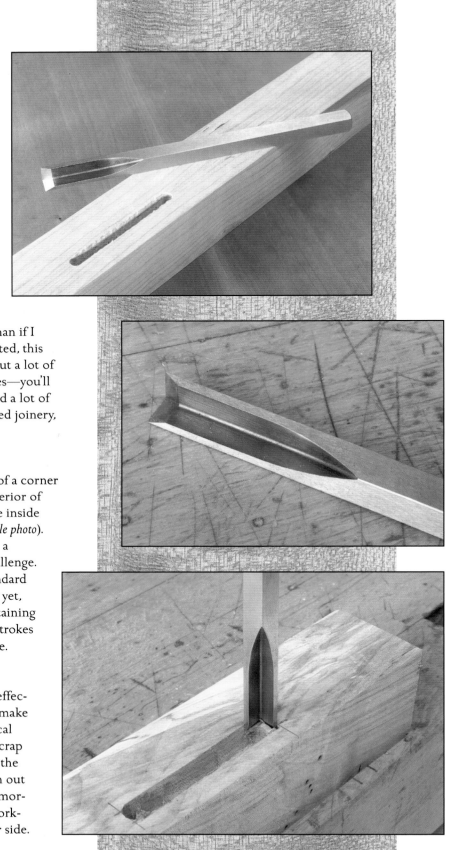

JAPANESE CHISELS

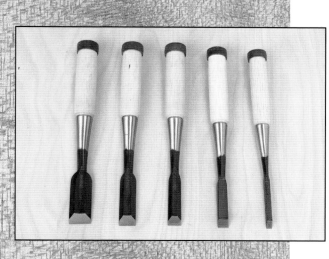

My Japanese chisels are absolutely a joy to use. With their wood handles and short blades, they balance perfectly in my hand. The special laminated-steel construction creates a blade that is easy to sharpen yet maintains a keen edge (*top photo*). How can they offer so much in such a small package? For starters, the construction of Japanese chisels differs considerably from that of their Western cousins.

Bi-metal blades

Unlike the blade of a Western chisel, which is forged from a single piece of steel, a Japanese chisel is made from two distinct layers that are forge-welded together (*middle drawing*). The lower layer is a high-carbon steel that's very hard (typically Rc 60 to 65). Although this can maintain a razor edge, it's quite brittle. So a mild low-carbon layer is welded on top of it to support the brittle metal by absorbing impact. The backs of the chisels are often hollowed out in the center to make flattening easier.

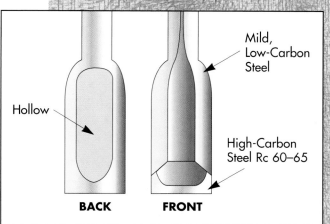

Mild, Low-Carbon Steel

Hollow

High-Carbon Steel Rc 60–65

BACK   **FRONT**

Basic use

Most Japanese chisels have ferrules on each end of the handle to prevent splitting (*bottom drawing*). Since the blades are stout and the handles are short, even a bevel-edged Japanese chisel can take the punishment of repeated blows from a mallet or Japanese hammer (*see page 147*). There is a huge range in quality and cost for Japanese chisels. If you're starting out, I'd advise beginning with a less-expensive set.

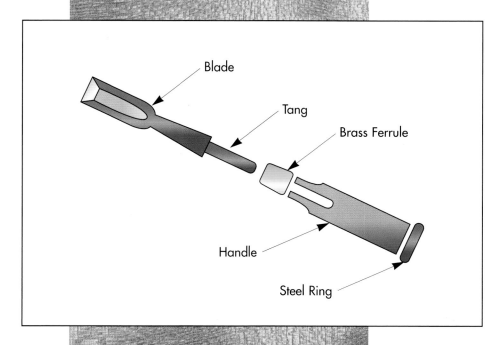

Blade

Tang

Brass Ferrule

Handle

Steel Ring

SPOKESHAVES

Although a spokeshave is technically a type of plane, I've included it in this chapter because it's most often used for shaping. A spokeshave is really a double-handled plane with a very short sole (*top photo*). This short sole is what allows the spokeshave to navigate curves that an ordinary plane couldn't handle. There are a number of spokeshaves available, the most common being the flat-bottomed sole. This is a good, all-purpose shaping tool. Other specialty spokeshaves include those with a curved sole from front to back, and those with soles that are either concave or convex. I've found the specialty spokeshaves to be of limited use, as the blades are quite time-consuming to sharpen.

Originally designed to shape spokes for wagon wheels, spokeshaves still find a home in many shops today. I use mine when I shape cabriole legs (*middle photo*), add a chamfer to a curved edge, or need a round-over on a curved part. In use, a firm grip is essential, and the tool may be either pushed or pulled. I generally prefer to pull because this gives better control.

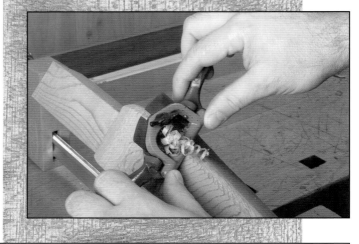

Adjustable blades

When you're shopping for a spokeshave, I recommend the type with an adjustable blade. This type of spokeshave has a pair of knurled knobs that slip into slots in the blade to move it up and down as they're turned (*bottom drawing*). This also helps prevent the blade from shifting out of position in use. Plainer versions use a screw to hold the blade in place and are a pain to adjust.

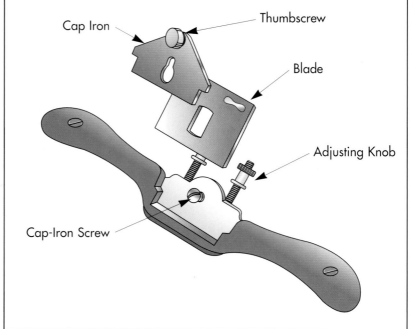

Cap Iron — Thumbscrew

Blade

Adjusting Knob

Cap-Iron Screw

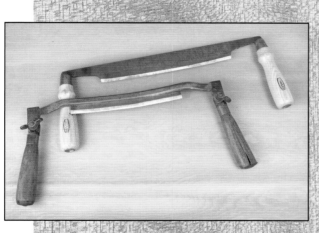

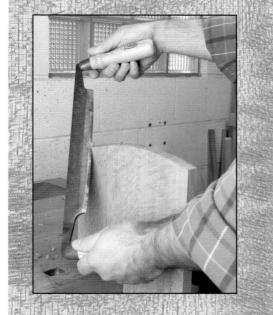

DRAWKNIVES

Many woodworkers will never use a drawknife (*top photo*). It's a big, exposed blade, and the cut is totally hand-controlled. But in the hands of a skilled craftsman, it can do amazing things. I had the pleasure of sitting in on a class with master chairmaker Brian Boggs and was simply amazed at what he could do with just a drawknife and a spokeshave. He makes exquisite chairs that are as comfortable as they are beautiful. And he personally guarantees that they'll outlast the owner.

A drawknife is basically a long, thin blade with tangs on the ends that are bent to fit into wood handles (*bottom drawing*). The blade can be straight or curved, and handles are long and straight, turned, or even small knobs. On my great-grandfather's drawknife (*bottom drawknife in top photo*), the handles are adjustable: They can be turned in toward the blade to protect the edge and allow it to slip more easily into a toolbox.

There's a lot of debate over using a drawknife with the bevel up versus down. I say, use what feels best; experiment to find which gives you better control. As with many other tools, a skewed cut will produce more of a shearing cut to cleanly cut wood fibers (*middle photo*). In my opinion, the big challenge to a drawknife is sharpening one. Start by flattening the back: Rub a sharpening stone on the back of the drawknife in small, circular strokes. If the bevel needs reshaping, it may be easier to use a portable belt sander than a grinding wheel. Honing is best done by rubbing the stone on the blade instead of the blade on the stone.

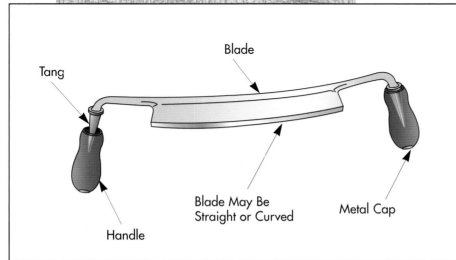

Blade

Tang

Blade May Be
Straight or Curved

Metal Cap

Handle

CARVING TOOLS

The first time I seriously began shopping for carving tools, I couldn't help snickering at some of the names: Fluteroni, spoon bit, allongee fishtail? Silly though they may sound, these names have special meaning to carvers, and often aptly describe the business end of the tool. Carving tools can be broadly categorized into three main groups: gouges, chisels, and specialty tools (*top photo*). Each tool is designed to handle a specific task; serious carvers can have dozens of carving tools, ranging from delicate 4"-long detail chisels to huge gouges for roughing-out work.

Standard sizes

Unlike most woodworking tools, carving tools have long been available in standard sizes (*bottom drawing*). If one carver tells another that he used a No. 8 gouge, the other will know exactly which tool he used. Surprisingly, most toolmakers follow these standards. Not all do, however, so stick with a reputable brand when you buy.

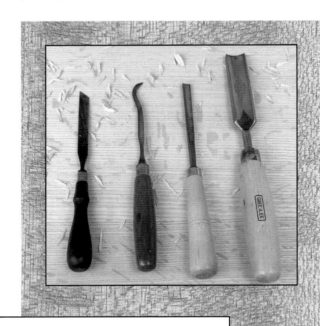

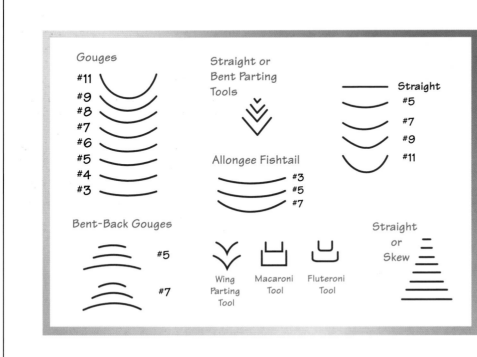

Gouges

A carving gouge is basically a chisel that's curved across the width of the blade (*top photo*). Of all the carving tools, you'll find that gouges have the widest array of curves, sizes, and special features (such as a bent neck). In general, gouges may be one of two types: in-cannel or out-cannel. With an in-cannel gouge, the bevel is ground on the inside of the blade; an out-cannel gouge has its bevel ground on the outside. Out-cannel gouges are by far the more popular.

Chisels

Although some carving chisels often look similar to standard firmer chisels, there's one big difference: Instead of the bevel being ground on one side, the bevel on a carving chisel is ground on both sides so it'll meet in the center (*middle photo*). Unlike the concave (hollow) grind of most chisels, a carving chisel generally has a convex grind. This helps prevent the edge from digging in too deep in use. Carving chisels may have either a square edge or a skewed edge.

Specialty tools

In addition to gouges and chisels, the carver typically has a number of other specialty tools in his arsenal (*bottom photo*). Parting tools and veiners are the standbys. The most commonly used parting tool is the V-shaped version used for cutting grooves in wood and making square-cornered cuts. The V-parting tool is widely used for incising letters in signs. Veiners can have square or rounded edges and are used mainly to add decorative grooves or "veins" in carvings.

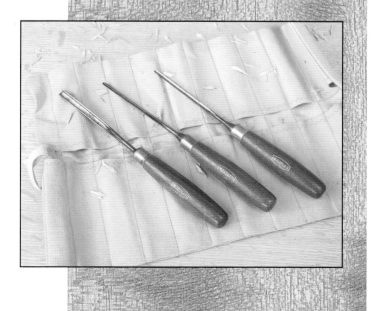

FILE & RASP TERMINOLOGY

How often you use files and rasps will depend heavily on the type of work you do and how long you've been woodworking. If your work involves a lot of curved shapes, your files and rasps are likely very prominent in your tool cabinet. Folks who build antique reproductions, especially Queen Anne furniture, with its classic S-shaped cabriole legs, use files and rasps regularly. On the other hand, if you build Craftsman-style furniture, with its rectilinear lines, you probably use them less.

How long you've been woodworking is also a factor. I used files and rasps much more often when I was a novice than I do now. This was partly because I didn't have as many tools then, and also that I've since learned better ways to do the jobs. Now, for example, instead of trying to fit a tenon into a mortise by filing it, I use a shoulder plane or a chisel. And instead of shaping a curve on a leg with a file, I tend to use a spokeshave. Any of these tools leaves a cleaner, smoother surface than a file or rasp and, just as important, is more of a pleasure for me to use. I still use my rasps and files—just not as often.

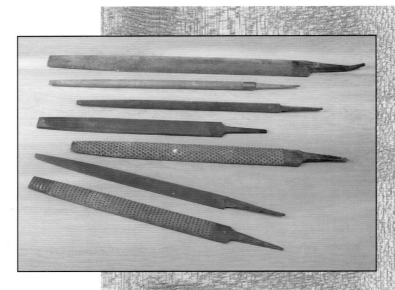

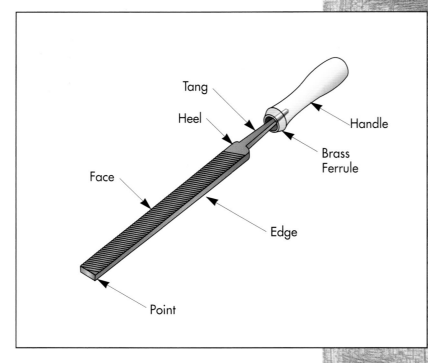

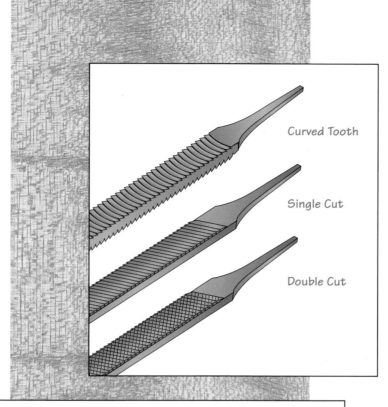

Curved Tooth

Single Cut

Double Cut

File cuts

Files are made by cutting parallel rows of teeth into the surface of the metal at an angle (usually between 60 and 80 degrees). There are three common "cuts" available: single cut, double cut, and curved tooth (*top drawing*). Single-cut files are the most common and work well for both general-purpose woodworking and the occasional metalworking I need to do around the shop. Double-cut files have a second set of teeth at an oppo-site angle to the first set; so they're more aggressive and work great when you need to remove a lot of material in a hurry. Curved-tooth files are becoming quite rare and are very aggressive. These have been replaced primarily by the rasp (*see page* 133).

Shapes

Files come in a huge variety of shapes and sizes. The most frequent shapes you'll find are: mill (or flat), half-round, round, 4-in-hand, and triangular (*bottom drawing*). For all-around woodworking, the half-round shape is your best bet. This combina-tion of a gently curving face with a flat face will handle most jobs. Lengths for files vary from 4" to 12" and larger. Eight-inch and 10" files are the most suitable for the shop, while smaller files, particularly taper or triangular files, are useful for sharpening.

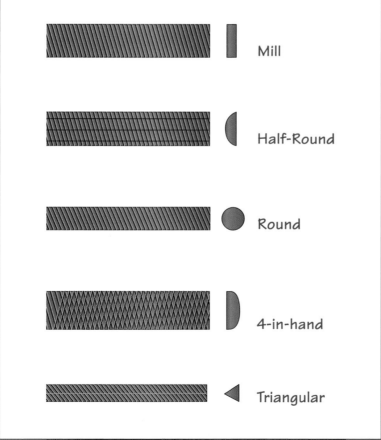

Mill

Half-Round

Round

4-in-hand

Triangular

MILL FILES

There are three common techniques for using a file: straight, cross-filing, and draw-filing. Each has advantages and disadvantages.

Straight

Straight or in-line filing is not used often, since most files perform best when skewed at an angle (*see Cross-filing, below*). There are times when in-line filing is your only option or actually works best for the job. When I prepare the edge of a scraper by filing it flat, I typically use the in-line method, since this helps to create an absolutely flat edge (*top photo*). If you hold the file at an angle, there's a big tendency to tip or rock the file, which will produce an angled cut.

Cross-filing

Cross-filing is the most common technique used with both files and rasps. With this method, the file is skewed at an angle to produce more of a shearing cut (*middle photo*). Cross-filing lets you quickly remove wood while leaving a fairly smooth surface. Any roughness can usually be removed with draw-filing (*see below*), a scraper, or sanding.

Draw-filing

Draw-filing puts the smoothest finish you can get on a surface with a file. The file is held at 90 degrees to the edge and is drawn across the surface (*bottom photo*). This technique works best with single-cut files and with a light touch. As with any filing operation, make sure to lift the file at the end of the stroke and return it to the starting position.

It's amazingly easy to destroy hours (even days) of work with one careless slip of a file. Since these beasts are all-metal, they can and will scratch, ding, and mar wood surfaces if allowed. Here's a tip that can save you a lot of aggravation when filing, particularly near surfaces that are easily damaged, such as plywood and veneered panels: Simply wrap a turn or two of masking or duct tape around the end of the file (*top photo*). This way you can safely rub the file on your surface without risk of damage.

FILE HANDLES

■ It's odd: Although almost every file manufacturer warns you not to use their files without a handle, none of them supply one. It's sort of like buying a table saw that doesn't come with a blade guard; go figure. The point is, you really should use a handle when using a file, because the tang is a rather nasty bit of work. It's sharp, often covered with burrs, and generally painful to hold in your hand. I admit that some of my files don't have handles, but I have taken the time to remove any burrs and soften the edges.

My example notwithstanding, it's a good idea to fit every file and rasp that you own with its own handle. These can be bought for little at most hardware stores, or you can easily make your own. If you're a turner, you can get fancy (*drawing below*). Otherwise, a short length of dowel will do—anything is better than nothing. NOTE: To prevent the handle from splitting, it's a good idea to add a metal ferrule; a short length of brass or copper pipe works great for this.

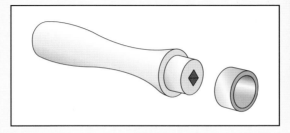

SPECIALTY FILES

Taper files

Taper-cut files are triangular-shaped files that taper along their length (*top photo*). They come in various sizes that are defined by their cross section and taper, not by their coarseness. Common sizes are regular, slim, extra slim, and double-extra slim. These files are most often used for sharpening saws but can be pressed into service for other tasks as well.

Needle files

Needle files (sometimes called jeweler's files) are thin, delicate files that are used for small, fine detail work. They're usually sold in sets that include a variety of shapes, including round (often called a rat-tail file), square, rectangular, half-round, triangular, and flat (*middle photo*). I use my needle files frequently to smooth tiny details, enlarge a hinge hole, and in the past, to sharpen spurs on some of my drill bits; this task has since been taken over by my diamond hones (*page* 137).

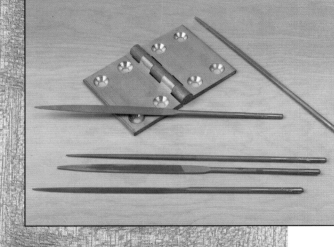

Riflers

Riflers are specialty files used primarily by carvers to smooth out small details in their work (*bottom photo*). They may be double-ended or come with a handle. Riflers are available individually or in sets and can be either files or rasps. I bought a set years ago when I first became interested in carving. Although I don't do a lot of carving anymore, I occasionally pull them out when I just can't get into a spot with any other tool. They really are quite handy.

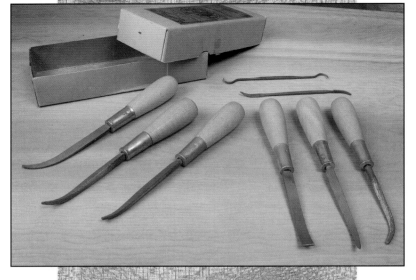

RASPS

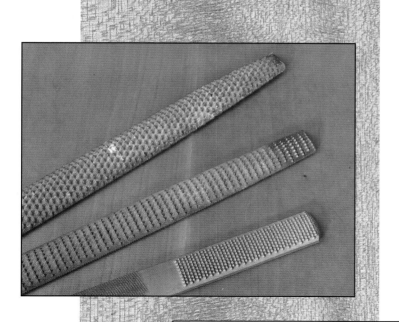

Even though rasps closely resemble files, they're very different beasts (*top photo*). Instead of single rows of teeth cut into the metal surface at an angle, rasps have tiny individual teeth in parallel rows. And unlike the smooth, almost planing action of a file, a rasp is designed to virtually tear out chucks of wood. This makes them very aggressive, and a rasp in the hands of a seasoned user can remove a lot of material in no time flat. That's why rasps are reserved solely for roughing-out work that will eventually be smoothed with files, scrapers, or sandpaper.

Most rasps are around 8" to 12" long and come in coarse, bastard, second-cut, and smooth grades. You may also see them described as either a wood rasp, a cabinet rasp, or a patternmaker's rasp (*bottom drawing*). Wood rasps are the most aggressive of these and usually come with a bastard cut in either flat or half-round profiles. Cabinet rasps are typically second-cut or smooth and also come in half-round and flat (half-round being the more common). Patternmaker's rasps are also available in second-cut and smooth, and they generally have smaller teeth that tend to leave a smoother finish than the cabinet rasp.

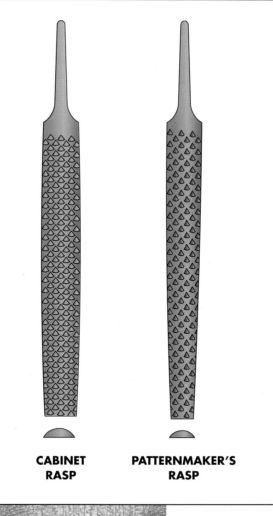

CABINET RASP

PATTERNMAKER'S RASP

One of my favorite rasps is a 4-in-hand rasp (originally called a shoe rasp). This handy tool combines four tools in one, as you'd guess from the name. It's doubled-ended with a half-round shape. One end is a rasp, the other a file—you'd think they'd call it a 4-in-hand rasp/file. Effectively, you have a half-round file, a flat file, a half-round rasp, and a flat rasp. What I like best about this tool is that both edges are "safe," or smooth. This makes the 4-in-hand rasp particularly useful when rounding-over tenons to fit into rounded-end mortises, like those cut by a router (*top drawing*).

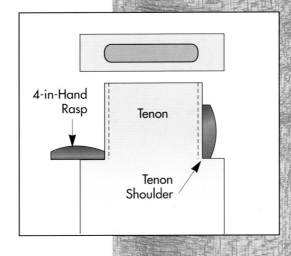

I also like how the shorter body fits nicely into my hand—and my shop apron pocket, too. My only use for this tool is light work, like fitting a joint or rounding-over tenons (*middle photo*). If I have a lot of wood to remove or I'm working on a long or large surface, I'll pull out the appropriate standard-length file or rasp, since the short body of the 4-in-hand is inadequate for this type of work.

FILECARDS

■ Files and rasps require a lot of maintenance—a lot more than some woodworkers give them. No wonder the tool skips over the surface instead of cutting properly. Most often it just needs to be cleaned, and you should do this after every half-dozen strokes or so. I know a lot of folks who've never cleaned their files. The problem is, the tiny teeth of a file

quickly fill with waste. If you don't remove it, the file can't work properly. Here's where a filecard comes into play (*photo at left*). Filecards typically have two faces: a nylon brush on one face and a wire brush on the other. Start with the nylon brush, and if this doesn't clean the file, flip it over and use the wire side. Stubborn bits can be removed with the steel pick that's commonly built into most filecards.

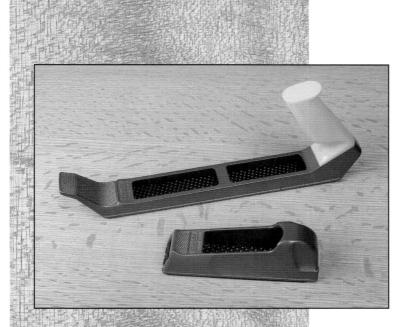

RASP PLANES

I know quite a few woodworkers who enjoy using a rasp plane. Rasp planes are commonly referred to by their trade name, Surform (a Stanley registered trademark). Surforms come in several shapes and sizes (*top photo*), but all use the same cutting plate. This is a steel plate with rows of small teeth pressed into the surface. When dull, the plate is discarded and a new one installed. The big advantage that this design offers over conventional rasps is that the teeth are a lot less likely to clog, since the waste can escape through the holes in the plate (*middle photo*).

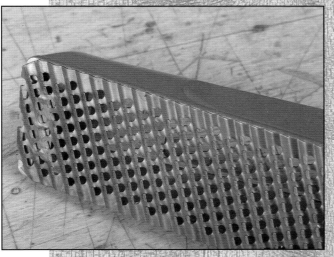

Surforms are intended for rough shaping, and they work well at this. I prefer other tools such as a drawknife or spokeshave, but my kids have always found Surforms very accessible. Each of them has whiled away hours in the shop with me, reducing a square scrap into a convoluted object that when "finished" was proudly proclaimed to be rocket ship, doll, or doggy (although most ended up looking like hotdog buns).

Basic use

Naturally, if young kids can use one of these, Surforms are simple to operate. Hold the tool much as you would a jack plane or block plane, and use even pressure as you shape (*bottom photo*). You'll find that the tooth design allows you to cut both with and against the grain, leaving a rough surface. Once rough shaping is done, final smoothing is essential.

SANDVIK FILES

I was skeptical the first time I read the package on a Sandvik file I was considering purchasing. If the file was only half as good as they promised, it'd be worth the money. According to the package, here was a nifty product that would virtually replace both the files and the sandpaper in my shop. Although this certainly hasn't happened, the Sandvik files that I've bought over the years have found a home in my tool cabinet (*top photo*).

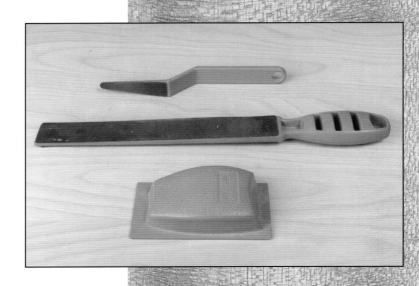

Tiny holes

Sandvik files (and other abrasive tools, like their sanding block), are all faced with a special steel plate that has a series of holes punched in the surface to replicate a variety of abrasive grits. What makes this work is that the holes are punched in the metal with great accuracy. And unlike sandpaper, which wears quickly, the sanding plates last considerably longer. When they do wear out, you can purchase a replacement plate.

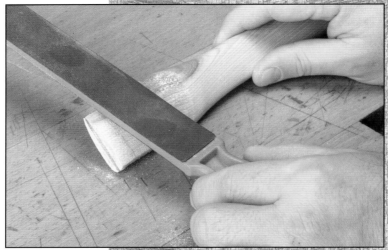

Basic use

Unlike standard files, Sandviks don't have to be pushed or pulled in one direction. You can literally move these in any direction and they'll cut (*middle photo*). This makes them particularly handy when working in tight quarters. The only secrets to using these are to let the sanding plate do the work, and to clean them often by rapping the tool against the side of your bench.

DIAMOND FILES/HONES

Several years ago, I was wandering around a woodworking show with a couple of dollars burning a hole in my pocket, when I saw a man demonstrating diamond hones. Seemed like a heck of an idea to me, so I bought a couple of flat pocket hones and a small set of diamond files (*top photo*) and took them home to try. What a discovery. I use these little guys all the time for everything from tuning a plane to sharpening a router bit. I'm on my second set of paddles, and the files are still in good shape.

Diamond hones and files are basically pieces of high-grade plastic with crushed industrial-quality diamond particles bonded to the surface. Many shapes and sizes are available (*middle drawing*), and they typically come in fine, medium, and coarse grits. Without a doubt, I use the paddle-style hones the most often (*bottom photo*). There are two things that make these so great. First, since the abrasive is diamond, it lasts a long time. Second, their diminutive size allows them to access places other stones can't reach, such as the short bed of a block plane. Diamond hones and files can be used dry or else with water as a lubricant. Since I'm usually removing only a small amount of metal with one of these, a lubricant is unnecessary.

"A woodworker's hands develop in a special way with intense and concentrated use. The flesh becomes stronger and heavier in certain areas, better fitted to grasp and use the tools."

GEORGE NAKASHIMA (1981)

ASSEMBLY TOOLS

Hammers, drills, screwdrivers, mallets; not the sexiest array of tools in the shop, but these essentials are, well, essential. There may be more types of all of these than you're familiar with, and it's an advantage to know both what's available and how to use it for maximum results. These deceptively mundane implements are easy to take for granted. They're everywhere, everyone knows how to use them (or think they do), and one is as good as the next, right? Actually, there are differences in quality, function, and use that can all make a difference in your completed piece.

For example, if you drive in brads with a claw hammer instead of a Warrington hammer, you'll smash your fingers and put dimples in the wood. And if you install brass hinge screws with an incorrect-sized screwdriver, you'll shred the screws and damage the hardware. So often, these assembly tools are the ones that bring the piece together in its final stage. They're the ones you reach for to install drawers, or attach doors. This is not the place for a bargain-bin, one-size-fits-all tool. This is where, as master woodworker Nakashima knew, you want to "grasp and use" the right one for the job.

Top left to bottom right: cast-iron hand drill made by Millers Falls Tool Co.; 10" flat-blade screwdriver; hardwood mallet with cast-iron rings; riveting hammer made by Warner & Noble; unplated beech brace; 9" combined round/flat-blade screwdriver; 4½" flat-blade screwdriver; 28-oz. forged claw hammer made by Warner & Noble.

HAMMER TERMINOLOGY

Although I rarely use nails in my woodworking projects, I do use hammers regularly. I'll pick one up to drive in wood pegs, tap parts together, and drive chisels (with my Japanese hammer). In addition to my favorite Japanese hammer, I use a couple of different weights of claw hammers, two sizes of Warrington hammer for driving in brads, and a ball-peen hammer for metalworking (*top photo*).

Regardless of the type, virtually all hammers are similar in construction (*bottom drawing*). This simple tool consists of a handle and head, and depending on the type of handle, one or more wedges to keep the head secured. Wood handles (like the one shown in the drawing below) typically have three wedges: one wood and two metal. The wood wedge spreads the sides of the tenon to grip the head, and the metal wedges help distribute the pressure evenly.

Metal handles are often forged along with the head and therefore will never loosen. Composite handles (fiberglass or other plastic composition) are usually secured to the head with high-grade epoxy. Although these have much less chance of loosening compared to a wood handle, they can break free from the head under heavy use.

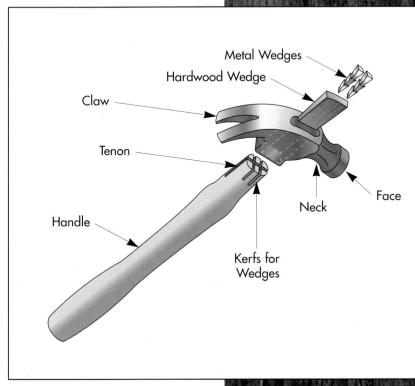

Metal Wedges

Hardwood Wedge

Claw

Tenon

Handle

Neck

Face

Kerfs for Wedges

CLAW HAMMERS

When most folks envision a hammer, they think of a claw hammer. And many believe a claw hammer is a claw hammer, right? Not true. There many different kinds of claws hammers available. For the most part, they can be divided into two types: those with curved claws, and those with straight claws (*top drawing*). Curved-claw hammers are by far the most common, and they are particularly adept at removing nails. Straight-claw hammers are more common in construction work, where the straighter claws are commonly used to pry parts apart. What a straight-claw hammer gains in demolition work, it loses in nail-pulling efficiency.

But there's more to claw hammers than the curve of the claw. The weight and handle (*see the sidebar below*) will also have a huge impact on how well the hammer performs. Weights range from a delicate 7 ounces up to a beefy 28 ounces; the most common is 16 ounces. Heavier hammers are mostly used in construction by experienced framers, who can drive a 16d nail into a 2-by in two or three strokes. A heavy hammer will drive nails faster, but it will also wear you out faster; these industrial-strength tools are best left to professionals.

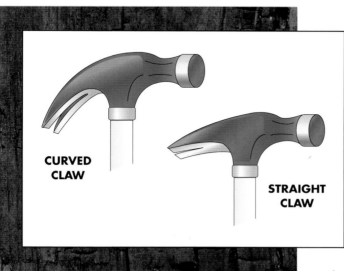

CURVED CLAW

STRAIGHT CLAW

HANDLE OPTIONS

Hammer handles have come a long way from the old hickory handles of my grandfather's hammer (*photo at right*). That's not to say wood handles aren't still used. They're still very popular, especially hickory because of its excellent flexibility and shock-absorbing characteristics. The big disadvantage to a wood handle is simply that it's wood—and wood constantly reacts to changes in humidity. Over time, the handle will loosen and need to be tightened or replaced. Wood handles can also fray and split under heavy use.

So it's no surprise that hammer manufacturers have been looking for a better handle. Two popular material choices are metal and fiberglass (or some other plastic composite). Both of these hold up better under heavy use, and rarely if ever

do they loosen inside the head. An interesting new entry by Stanley (www.stanleyworks.com) is their AntiVibe hammer. It features a one-piece, steel-forged design with a unique "tuning fork" shaft that greatly decreases harmful vibrations.

Even experienced woodworkers tend to hold a hammer with a weak grip. The most common mistake is to choke up on the handle as if it were a baseball bat (*top photo*). And just as with a baseball bat, this will rob the hammer of any power, greatly reducing its ability to drive a nail. Some might say that this affords better control; but without power, the hammer is useless. It's better to learn to control the hammer with the proper grip.

Handshake grip

To get the maximum mechanical advantage from a hammer, you need to grip the handle near the end (*middle photo*). Place the end of the handle in the meaty part of your palm, and wrap your fingers around the handle. Stay away from a white-knuckle grip, as this will only tire your hand. For less power and a bit more control, position the handle just below the palm, and grip. This takes the hammer out of alignment with your arm and shoulder, but you may find it more comfortable.

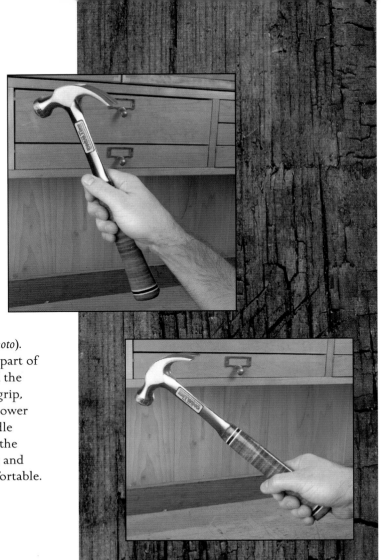

PULLING OUT NAILS

Even with the correct grip and stance, you'll occasionally hammer in a nail crooked or in the wrong place. Pulling out nails in a woodworking project is a bit different than in carpentry. With carpentry you generally don't care about dents in the surface of a 2×4. On a finished or near-finished woodworking project, this could be disastrous.

Here are two quick ways to avoid dents caused by the hammer. One way is to slip a scrap of wood under the head of the hammer to keep it from crushing the surface as it's pivoted to pull out the nail (*top photo at left*). A similar method that works particularly well for stubborn nails is a slotted wedge. The wedge creates better leverage while at the same time protecting the surface (*bottom photo at left*).

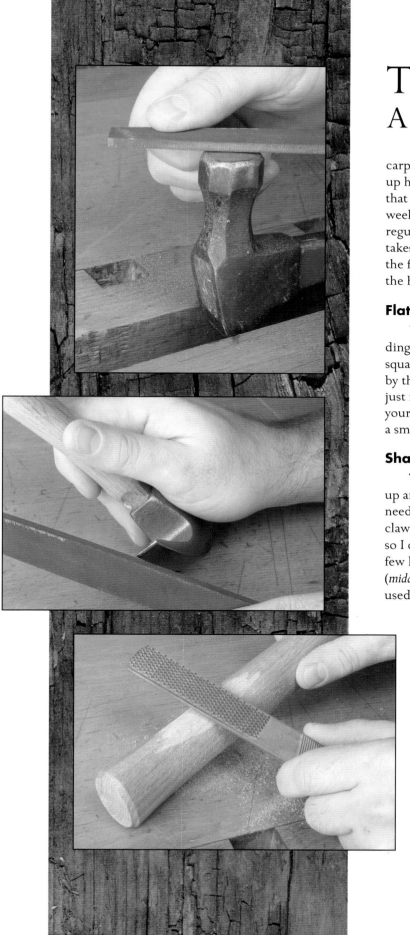

TUNING A HAMMER

I learned to "tune" a hammer from an old carpenter. It was something he'd do as he packed up his tools every Friday. Although it's unlikely that you'll need to tune your hammers once a week as he did, it's a good idea to inspect them regularly and tune them when needed. This takes only 5 minutes and consists of flattening the face, sharpening the claws, and maintaining the handle.

Flattening the face

With use, the face of a hammer tends to get dinged up. This makes it difficult to hit a nail squarely on the head. Also the "pockets" created by the dings can collect rust and other gunk. It just makes sense to routinely flatten the face of your hammers by taking a few light strokes with a smooth mill file (*top photo*).

Sharpening the claws

The claws on a hammer will also get dinged up and worn over time. There are two areas that need attention. First, since I often drive the claws of the hammer into a 2×4 when framing so I can lift it, I like to keep the ends sharp. A few licks with a file will bring back a sharp edge (*middle photo*). The inside edges of the claws are used to "bite" into nails to pull them. You can sharpen these edges by rocking the head of the hammer on sandpaper.

Handle

What you do to a handle will depend on what it's made of. All handles should be cleaned regularly to remove pitch and dirt. Wood handles will benefit from an occasional coat of oil. Also, don't hesitate to shape a wood handle to better fit your hand (*bottom photo*). Go over metal handles lightly with an emery cloth to remove any rust. Follow this with a light coat of machine oil. Little can be done with composite handles except regular cleaning.

REPLACING A HANDLE

Over time, the handle on a hammer can get cracked or break. Fortunately, it's easy to replace a handle—as long as it's sized correctly. I suggest taking the old hammer head with you to the hardware store or home center when you shop for a replacement. Or make one yourself; use the old handle as a pattern. Before you can install the replacement handle, of course, you'll need to remove the old one. Just saw it off near the head and then drive out the waste with a punch or large bolt.

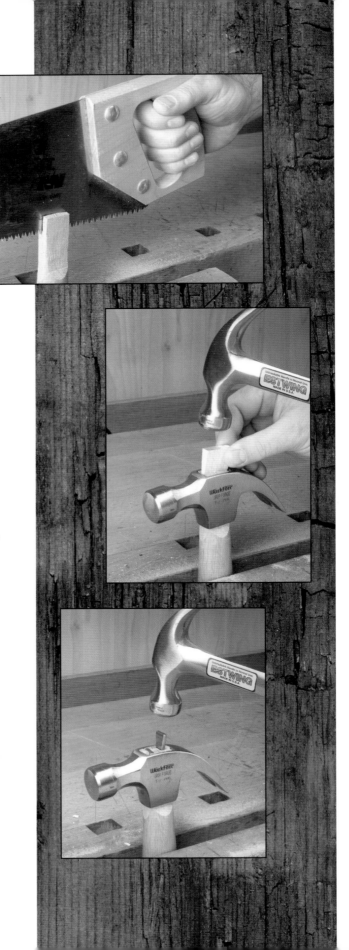

Cut kerfs

To ready the handle for the head, you'll first need to fit the tenon. A file will make quick work of this. Work around the tenon, removing the same amount on all four sides until the tenon slips into the head all the way and the shoulder bottoms out. Once the fit is good, mark and cut off the waste that protrudes above the head. Then remove the handle and cut three kerfs in the end. Cut a lengthwise kerf for a wood wedge, and two kerfs across the width for metal wedges (*top photo*).

Drive in wedges

Now you can slide the handle back in the head and install the large wood wedge. This wedge pushes the sides of the tenon out to grip the head. Don't be shy here—drive it in as far as it will go (*middle photo*). All that's left is to drive in the metal cross wedges that spread the tenon out evenly in the head (*bottom photo*). Drive these into the kerfs you cut earlier until they're flush with the head. That's it: You're ready to go.

Warrington Hammers

I have a couple of different sizes of Warrington hammers in my tool chest (*top photo*). These lighter-weight hammers are ideal for driving in finish nails and small brads. Instead of a claw, a Warrington hammer has a small, wedge-shaped cross peen that makes it especially useful for driving in brads. The cross peen is a real finger-saver when working with short, small brads (*middle photo*). Why? Because the cross peen will actually fit between my fingers to start the brad. Once it's started, I flip the hammer to use the flat face to drive in the brad. Another unique feature of this tool is the faces called "side strikes" on the sides of the hammer that let you drive nails in tight spaces.

Warrington hammers are available in four different weights: $3^{1}/_{2}$, 6, 10, and 12 ounces. I have a 6- and a 10-ounce hammer, and with these I can comfortably handle most tasks. There's something odd about these hammers: The end of the cross peen is either ground or cast to come to a point instead of being flat. This actually makes it difficult to start a brad, as the point will glance off the head of the brad. Try filing the point flat to make the tool a lot more usable.

NAIL SETS

One of the secrets to nailing effectively is knowing when to stop driving the nail with a hammer. The closer you get to the surface, the greater the chance of dinging it with the face of the hammer. To eliminate the chance of dings, stop when the head of the brad or nail nears the surface—usually $^{1}/_{16}$" to $^{1}/_{8}$". Then reach for a nail set (*photo at right*). A nail set is designed to finish the job by driving the nail below the surface, or "setting" it. Nail sets are available is various tip diameters; choose one that is closest to the diameter of the nail head. Place the set on the nail and tap it gently to set it below the surface. Keep a firm grip on the set, since it's easy for it to slip off and end up being driven into the wood.

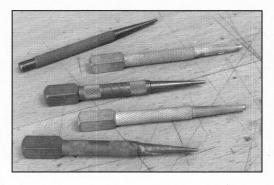

BALL-PEEN HAMMERS

Even though most of the work I do is in wood, I often find use for a ball-peen hammer (*top photo*). A ball-peen hammer is handy when I do need to work with metal—a material I often incorporate into jigs and fixtures. I also use a ball-peen hammer when I work with the metal hardware I install in many projects. A ball-peen hammer (sometimes called an engineer's hammer) has a standard flat face on one end and some type of peen on the other.

Head styles

There are three prevailing head styles for peened hammers: a straight peen, a cross peen, and by far the most common, the ball peen (*middle drawing*). Cross peens are popular on Warrington hammers, while straight peens are rarely seen outside of the metal shop. The rounded head of a ball-peen hammer is used mostly for riveting (*see the sidebar below*). Though I don't use a lot of rivets, I often peen brass rods over to attach brass parts to wood handles on some of the fine tools I make.

STRAIGHT PEEN

CROSS PEEN

BALL PEEN

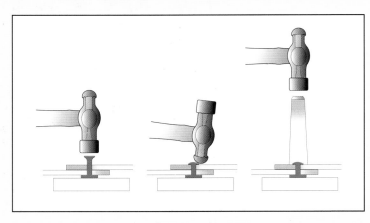

RIVETING

Riveting is a three-step process. First, a rivet is inserted through the parts to be joined, and the flat face of the hammer is used to "mushroom" the end of the rivet (*drawing at left*). Then, the hammer is flipped and the ball peen is used to further shape the rivet into a rough dome. Finally, a rivet set is used to create a smooth surface on the end.

Japanese Hammers

The first time I picked up a Japanese hammer, I knew I had to have one. Its compact head and sturdy handle gave it balance I'd never found in a Western hammer (*top photo*). The types of Japanese hammers you'll most likely find useful in your shop are the chisel hammers and the plane-adjusting hammers.

Chisel hammers

Chisel hammers may have one of two head styles: barrel or flat (*middle drawing*). The flat type are more common and are usually made of high-quality tool steel and then tempered to produce a tough, durable head. Since both faces are identical, the balance is near perfect. Some woodworkers prefer the barrel head–style chisel hammer; they feel that this more-compact design centers the weight closer to the handle, so they have greater control. These stubby heads are usually tempered so they're soft on the inside and hard on the inside. The theory is that this type of tempering reduces head "bounce."

POLISHING PLANE-ADJUSTING HAMMER **BARREL-SHAPED CHISEL HAMMER** **CHISEL HAMMER**

Plane-adjusting hammers

Plane-adjusting hammers can be identified by their thin, slender heads and brightly polished finish (*bottom photo*). Because of the degree of finish, these hammers are intended for use only on planes to adjust the cutters. Granted, you could use a different hammer for this task, but the face will probably be dinged or dented; these marks will transfer to the wood body of the plane—not a good way to treat a valuable tool.

BRAD DRIVERS

A brad driver is one of those "only" tools: When you need it, it's the only tool for the job. Brad drivers install brads and small nails by driving the brad into the wood itself—no hammer necessary. There are two basic types of brad drivers: a push-style driver that looks like an awl on steroids, and an odd-looking, hand-operated device that's sort of a cross between a small clamp and a nutcracker (*top photo*). The push-style driver works extremely well in tight quarters; framers (the picture variety) are partial to the hand-operated type.

Basic use

To use a push-style brad driver, insert the brad into the hollow barrel; a magnet inside holds it in place until it's driven in. Then place the tip where you want the brad and push. The spring-loaded barrel retracts up into the shaft while driving in the brad (*middle photo*). With the hand-operated type, you need to hold the brad in position with one hand and squeeze the handle with the other.

BLIND-NAILERS

Occasionally, you may need to nail a part in place where the head absolutely cannot show. You could set the brad and apply putty, but this is still visible. To do the job without leaving a trace, consider blind-nailing. With this technique, a tiny sliver of wood is peeled up from the surface to create a hiding place for the nail. The nail is driven in, the sliver is glued back down, and the nail disappears. The sliver can be peeled back with the corner of a chisel, or with a blind-nailer—sort of a tiny plane with a protruding blade (*photo above right*).

MALLETS

In addition to the various hammers I have in the shop, I also have a selection of mallets. Each is designed to tackle a different type of task. I have a joiner's mallet, a couple of different-sized dead-blow mallets, a rubber-faced mallet, and two sizes of carver's mallets.

Joiner's mallet

This was my original mallet. The catalog I ordered it from called it a joiner's mallet, and since I wanted to experience the wild world of joinery, it seemed like the tool for the job (*top photo*). To be honest, it never really felt right to me: It was (and still is) sort of clunky and large, and the flat, unforgiving faces of the mallet made it awkward to use. About the only thing I've used it for is driving a chisel. But since I picked up my Japanese hammer, this mallet's been relegated to the kids' toolbox.

Dead-blow mallet

What a great invention! Dead-blow mallets are high-impact plastic cases that enclose a head filled with oil and lead shot (*middle photo*). When the mallet strikes an object, the shot rushes to that end, but the thick oil prevents it from bouncing back. This delivers a "dead" blow with hardly any bounce. I have two sizes of these and use them more than my other mallets combined.

Rubber-faced mallet

A rubber-faced mallet is useful for those jobs where a different mallet or hammer would damage the surface. They typically come with interchangeable heads that screw on and off (*bottom photo*). I use mine occasionally during final assembly of parts that have been prefinished.

Carver's mallet

Years ago when I got into carving, I bought a couple of hardwood carver's mallets. Each was turned from a single piece of lignum vitae (one of the toughest woods known), and they're still in great shape even after lots of use. Carver's mallets are identified by their round head, which allows a carver to work from almost any angle without having to change his grip on the tool. These mallets tend to be heavy so that the carver can transfer a lot of power to the chisel. Newer carver's mallets have a wood body and handle but are wrapped in a thick layer of high-impact plastic (*top photo*). I have a carver friend who swears by his, but I just can't get past the plastic part—it just doesn't sit right with me. I'll stick with my lignum vitae.

MALLET GRIPS: FULL AND PARTIAL

There are two main grips that you can use with almost any mallet: full and partial. With a full grip, your hand wraps around the handle and the tool is used much like a hammer to deliver a full-force blow (*photo below left*). When you need a more delicate touch, switch to a partial grip, where your hand wraps around the head of the mallet (*photo below right*). Gripping a mallet this way robs it of power but gives much greater control.

 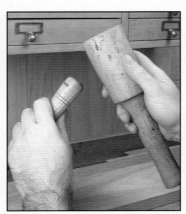

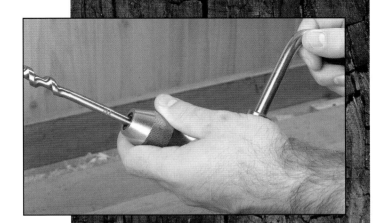

BRACES

Until I bought my first electric drill in 1971, I drilled all my holes with the brace shown in the top photo and the hand drill on page 152. And I drilled a lot of holes with these two guys. I don't use them much anymore except when I make something entirely by hand, but I still hang onto them. Braces have been around for a long time, but they have almost disappeared since the advent of the electric drill and now the cordless drill.

It might surprise you to know that many installers (cable TV, telephone, etc.) still use a brace. Why? The answer is feedback. The power of an electric drill can also be a detriment: An electric drill and a sharp bit will blow through most materials in a heartbeat. Installers use a brace because they can "feel" the bit moving through a wall. If they hit metal, they'll know it. This is important if you are interested in not drilling through electrical conduit, gas lines, or water lines.

Most of the bits used with this style brace have a square tang (*see page* 153) that's gripped by the jaws of the chuck. To insert or remove a bit, grasp the chuck with one hand and rotate the frame to open or close the jaws (*middle photo*). Quality braces have a ratcheting mechanism that allows you to turn the chuck in a confined space (*bottom drawing*).

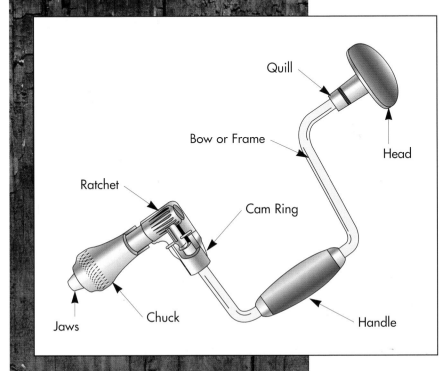

Quill

Bow or Frame

Head

Ratchet

Cam Ring

Jaws

Chuck

Handle

HAND DRILLS

I've always enjoyed using a hand drill—the cranking motion reminds me of my Mom's egg beater. The hand drill (sometimes called a wheel brace) is designed to accept twist bits (*see page* 153), so it's used to drill small holes compared to the larger holes possible with a brace. One of the things I like best about a hand drill is that it's very easy to vary the speed to match the material you're drilling. Inexpensive drills (like the one shown here) have only a single pinion to engage the larger drive gear (*bottom drawing*). Better-quality drills have two pinions to provide more reliable torque (my little single-pinion gear will often skip a tooth or two when it's pushed too hard, though that's not bad for a 30-year-old drill).

You insert or remove bits much the same way as with a brace. The only difference is, you need to prevent the drive gear from turning as you try to loosen or tighten the chuck. The best way I've found to do this is to wrap the index finger of the hand with which I'm holding the handle around the drive gear knob (*middle photo*). This does a pretty good job of freezing the drive gear so the chuck can be rotated. When using a hand drill, it's important to use a really sharp bit and to clear the waste frequently (*top photo*).

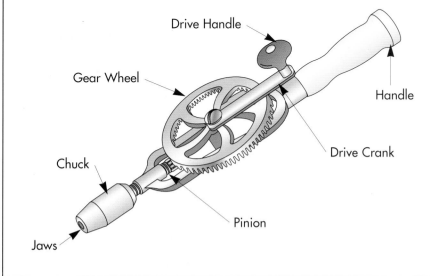

Drive Handle

Gear Wheel

Handle

Chuck

Drive Crank

Pinion

Jaws

BITS

There are two basic types of bits that work well with hand drills: auger bits for braces, and twist bits for hand drills.

Auger bits

There's quite a variety of auger bits still available (*top photo*). They can have the classic square tang or a round shank. The square tang variety will provide the better nonslip torque of the two. Auger bits also come in a couple of different twists: single and double. Double-twist bits have two flutes that run the length of the shaft and quickly clear out waste. A single-twist bit usually has a solid center. Although it doesn't clear waste as efficiently as the double-twist does, its solid core is much stronger—that's why you'll often see this style used on longer bits. A special type of auger bit called the expansive bit can be adjusted to drill a variety of diameters (*middle photo*). It comes with an adjustable cutter that slides in and out to change diameter.

Twist bits

Twist bits (or twist drills) are straight bits with two helix-type flutes running about two-thirds the length of the bit (*bottom photo*). This allows for excellent chip removal and leaves the end plain to fit in the drill chuck. The ends are typically ground to around a 60-degree bevel. This works fine for general-purpose work; but if you're intending to use a set just for woodworking, you may want to consider having them ground to a slightly steeper angle.

DRILLING TIPS

The rules for effective drilling are the same for a brace and a hand drill as they are for an electric drill. The bit needs to be guided in straight, and you need to take precautions to prevent tear-out. The big difference is, you need to do both of these while twirling the drill frame or knob. It takes a bit of practice, but it's quite enjoyable.

Drilling straight

There are a couple of simple, effective ways to ensure that the holes you drill end up straight. One method is to use a sight aid. A sight aid is nothing more than a try square or square block of wood that you position near the workpiece so that you can sight along it to keep the bit straight (*top photo*). Another method for drilling straight involves using a block of wood to support the bit and keep it running true. This is especially useful on long auger bits. Just start the hole and then stop and clamp a square scrap directly under the bottom of the hole. Then use the block to guide the bit (*middle photo*).

Preventing tear-out

If you drill completely through an unsupported workpiece, the bit will "blow out" the opposite face as it exits the wood. With twist bits, the best way to avoid this is to clamp a scrap block behind the workpiece to support the wood. You can use this same technique with auger bits, or stop drilling once the lead screw pokes out the back of the wood. Pull the drill out and continue drilling from the opposite face (*bottom photo*).

Screwdrivers

The final assembly tool that most woodworkers can't do without is the screwdriver. Flat-blade and Phillips are the most common, though square-drive screws are becoming increasingly popular with woodworkers, as their square recess provides an excellent grip. I have a nice set of wood-handled cabinetmaker's screwdrivers that I use exclusively for woodworking (*top photo*). Call me old-fashioned, but I still like the feel of a wood handle, especially the way the bulbous end fits so well in the palm of my hand.

That said, I do have a couple of those snappy combination screwdrivers with the pull-out double-ended shaft and reversible bits—the kind that has two different-sized Phillips and flat-blade tips. I use these for home improvement work and other non-wood-related jobs.

FITTING A BLADE: TOO WIDE, TOO NARROW, JUST RIGHT

The most common error when using a screwdriver is not sizing it properly to match the screw head. This is particularly true with slotted screws. When the screwdriver blade is too wide (*photo above near right*), the protruding edges of the screwdriver tip will most certainly damage the surrounding wood when it reaches the surface. If a blade is too narrow, it won't grip the screw fully and will most likely strip out (*photo above center*). A properly fit blade will fill the slot completely without extending past the perimeter of the head (*photo above right*).

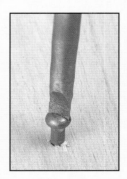

"In gluing the miters, it will be proper, first, to glue on the outside of each miter a piece of deal in the shape of a wedge, which will take a hand-screw, so that when they are putting together, the glue may be brought out, and the miters made close."

THOMAS SHERATON (1793)

CLAMPING TOOLS

Miter joints are notorious for clamping problems—and were obviously so in Mr. Sheraton's time, too. He didn't have some of our modern-day advantages, though, in the array of clamps available: spring clamps, C-clamps, bar clamps, Bessey's, hand screws, edge clamps, and more. It's an old saw in woodworking that happens to be true: You just can't have too many clamps. But you do need to have and use the right kind: If you have three dozen spring clamps but only two pipe clamps, you'll never be able to glue a panel successfully.

You also need to know when and how to use—and not over-use—the different types. When I first started woodworking, I'd try to compensate for a sloppy joint by cranking up the pressure on the biggest pipe clamp I could find. As one of my buddies would often say, "If the joint doesn't fit, get a bigger clamp." As you probably know, the wood will always win in the end. The solution is a two-parter: Concentrate a little more on your joinery skills, and then use the right clamp, with the right pressure, to help bring it all together.

Clockwise from top left: hand screw with self-aligning jaw made by Wm. H. Denny, patented 1887; cam-lock bar clamp, patented 1881; No. 1 cam-lock bar clamp, patented 1881; cabinetmaker's wooden bar clamp; cast-iron C-clamp; No. 2 cam-lock bar clamp; Dehne's automatic clamp heads, mounted on $7/8" \times 2^1/4"$ beam, marked "No 1, Pat 1886"; bar clamp made by Chicago Clamp Co., Chicago, patented 1893.

C-Clamps

C-clamps are one of the most universally used clamps in the shop (*top photo*). They're extremely versatile and are available in many sizes, with jaw capacities ranging from $^3/_4$" all the way up to a heavy-duty 12".

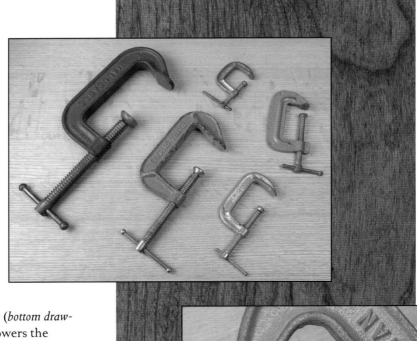

The C-shaped frame of the clamp has a fixed pad on one end and accepts a threaded screw on the other. One end of the screw accepts a swiveling shoe, while the other is pieced by a metal rod called a tommy bar (*bottom drawing*). Twisting the screw raises or lowers the shoe, thereby opening or closing the jaws of the clamps. The frames can be made of stamped metal, cast iron, steel, or aluminum. Tommy bars can be fixed or they may slide. On some C-clamps, the tommy bar is replaced with a wing-type thumbscrew.

One of the advantages of allowing the shoe to swivel is that it can conform to angled workpieces (*middle photo*). This same advantage can be troublesome when you're trying to fit a C-clamp on a narrow surface. In this case, you're usually better off flipping the C-clamp so the fixed jaw rests on the narrow piece. Consider what happens, for example, when you're trying to clamp a workpiece to a drill press table. Quite often the thin castings under the table are exactly where you need to apply the clamp (Murphy's Law in action). Just flip the clamp vertically so the fixed jaw rests on the casting, and it'll work fine. NOTE: C-clamps are intended for light to moderate pressure only; excessive pressure can crack the casting. If you need to exert greater force, go with a hand screw (*see page* 160) or a small bar clamp (*see page* 166).

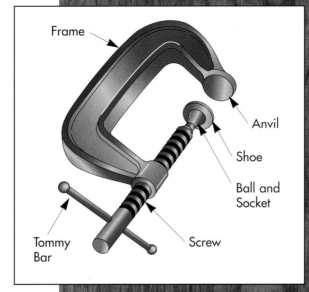

Frame

Anvil

Shoe

Ball and Socket

Tommy Bar

Screw

CLAMP TIPS

Spinning C-clamps

I picked this tip up as a young lad, when I watched a trim carpenter gluing up a laminated curve for a window sash. He was working with C-clamps, one in each hand, and was adjusting and applying them simultaneously. To open or close the jaws of a clamp, he'd hold the clamp by the screw and "spin" the body of the clamp, much like you'd twirl one of those old-time party favors that would make a clackety-clack noise (*top photo*). Try it—it really works.

Edge-clamping

Here's a good way to convert an ordinary C-clamp into an edge clamp for attaching edging to a workpiece. Position the clamp on the edge of the workpiece so there's roughly a 1/2" gap between the body of the clamp and the edging you're attaching (*middle photo*). Tighten the clamp securely and then tap a wedge in between the body of the clamp and the edging, as shown in the middle photo, until the edging is tight. Space the clamps about every 6" or so to ensure a good glue joint.

Square corners

C-clamps are handy for gluing up small projects like boxes and drawers, where larger clamps would be cumbersome. To make sure the corners glue up square, I use short lengths of aluminum or steel angle with the clamps to help align everything (*bottom photo*). Aluminum angle works best for this, since you don't have to worry about the metal interacting with the glue and causing stains. Make sure to file the ends of the angle smooth to keep from marring the work surface.

HAND SCREWS

Hand screws (sometimes called parallel clamps) have been around for centuries. Older versions used wood screws, while modern hand screws feature metal rods that thread into round nuts that can pivot, allowing for angled clamping (*top photo*). The jaws of hand screws are usually made of maple or birch and offer clamping capacities between 2" and 12". Although I've picked up many of the new clamps that have been introduced in recent years, I still regularly use my hand screws for clamping small parallel and irregular workpieces.

Parallel surfaces

One of the things I've always liked about hand screws is their ability to quickly clamp parallel surfaces. With a couple turns of the hand screw, you get it close to the size needed. To do this, grasp one handle with your right hand and the other with your left and then spin the clamp, rotating your wrists as if you were "pedaling" a bike. Open the jaws by pedaling forward, and close them by going backward (*middle drawing*). When the jaws will fit over the workpiece, alternately tighten one, then the other jaw (or tighten them at the same time) until the jaws are in full contact with the workpiece.

Irregular surfaces

More so than most other clamps, hand screws also excel at clamping irregular surfaces. That's because the jaws can be adjusted independently of each other. Here again, the idea is the same: You want to bring both jaws in full contact with the sides of the workpiece (*bottom photo*).

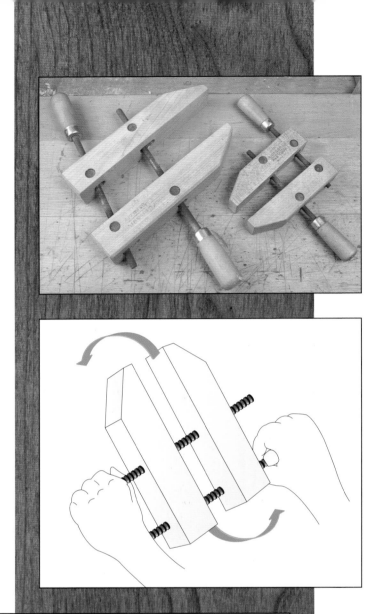

Specialty Clamps

Fast-action clamps

When fast-action clamps hit the market a few years ago, they created quite a stir. These clamps (sold under the Quick-Grip trade name) were designed to be used one-handed (*top photo*). Pressure is applied by squeezing the handle. To remove pressure, you pull a quick-release trigger. I find them extremely handy in the shop—more as a third hand than as a clamp—although I do occasionally use them to clamp parts together that require only light pressure. If you need greater clamping pressure, use a hand screw or a small bar clamp.

Spring clamps

Since the clamping pressure supplied by a spring clamp comes from a wire-wound spring, these small clamps are primarily used to hold small parts together under light pressure (*middle photo*). I routinely use them in the shop to apply a thin molding or edging strip to a workpiece. They're also handy for temporarily holding stops in place on a miter gauge or a rip fence. These small clamps tend to "creep" when used to glue parts together, and often work best in conjunction with C-clamps.

Band clamps

Band clamps (sometimes called strap or web clamps) are particularly useful for gluing up odd-shaped work such as an octagon. They can also be used to apply even pressure around a case or carcass (*bottom photo*) and are often used to glue up chairs and other non-square work. A band clamp consists of a cloth band or web that slips around the workpiece and is then threaded through the clamping head. A ratchet mechanism here allows you to apply considerable force. Clamping pressure is released by depressing the ratchet lever.

Photo courtesy of American Tool Companies, Inc., copyright 2001

PIPE CLAMPS

It's a rare woodworker's shop that doesn't have pipe clamps (*top photo*), and for good reason: They're hardworking and inexpensive. Pipe clamps are sold in single sets consisting of a separate head and tail piece (*middle drawing*). You supply the pipe, and that's one of the beauties of these clamps: They can be any length. You can buy pipe clamp heads that accept either $1/2$"- or $3/4$"-diameter pipe. The $1/2$"-diameter sets are suitable for light to moderate pressure, whereas the $3/4$" sets can supply a frightening amount of torque.

When I first started out, I figured that bigger is better, but now most of my pipe clamps are $1/2$". If you need the force supplied by the larger clamps, there's probably something wrong with the fit of the parts. It's best to pull these apart and tweak them to fit better. Some clamp sets are designed with "clutch" mechanisms on both heads. I'd steer clear of these and invest in the type that requires a threaded rod on the fixed jaw end.

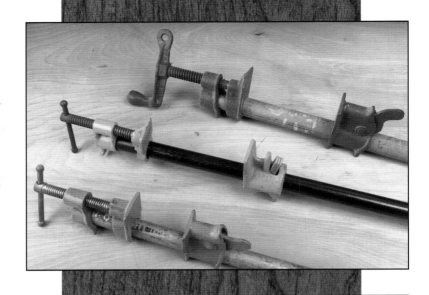

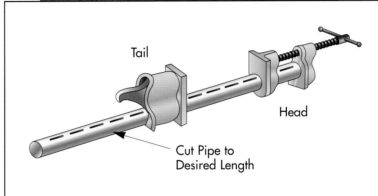

Tail

Head

Cut Pipe to
Desired Length

PIPE CLAMP PADS

Since pipe clamps can exert a lot of pressure, it's important to protect the workpiece from being marred by the metal clamp parts. The simplest way to do this is to add pads to the faces of the clamps. Store-bought pads, wood scraps, and plastic coating all work well for this (*photo below left*). Most clamp

manufacturers sell plastic pads specifically designed to fit their clamps. These slip right over the clamp and do a good job, although many have a tendency to fall off with use. Another method is to coat the pad faces with Plasti-Dip—a liquid plastic that hardens quickly when exposed to air (it's available at most hardware stores). Finally, the old standby is to apply scraps of wood ($1/4$" hardboards works great) to the jaw faces with double-sided tape.

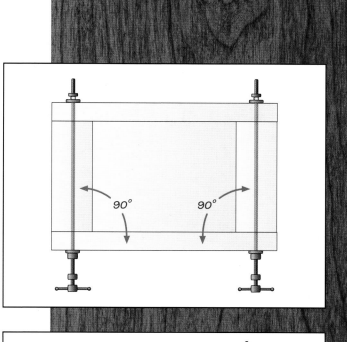

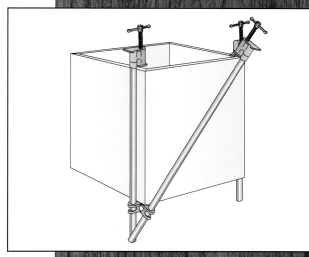

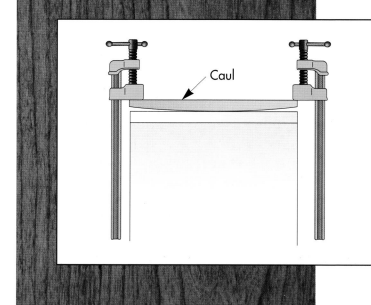

One of the challenges to using pipe clamps is aligning them so they'll pull parts together without causing them to shift or twist. The key is to position them so they're parallel to the sides of the workpiece (*top drawing*). I like to roughly position a clamp so it's friction-tight. Then I use a wood scrap to align the clamps by holding it flush with the edge of the workpiece; then I tap the clamp until it butts against the scrap. I do this for both ends, double-checking to make sure neither has shifted before I tighten the clamps.

Diagonals

Even with careful clamp positioning, a case often goes out of square under clamping pressure. The simplest way to check for this is to measure diagonally across the corners. If the measurements match, the corners are perfect 90's. Most likely they won't be. When this happens, attach a clamp across the longest measurement as shown in the middle drawing. Apply gentle pressure to "rack" the case back into square. Check the diagonals again and continue clamping until they're the same.

Using a caul

Pipe clamps are great at applying pressure at a single point, but they're not so hot at distributing pressure over a wide area. This can be a real problem when you're gluing up a case and need the pressure to spread over the entire length of a joint. Here's where a caul can come to the rescue. A caul is just a scrap of hardwood whose ends are tapered evenly away from the center (*bottom drawing*). In use, the ends of the caul are forced down with pipe clamps and the slight bow in the caul creates pressure all along the joint.

PIPE CLAMP TIPS

Double up clamps

Although most of my pipe clamps are 5 to 6 feet long, I occasionally come across a clamping job where they're too short. A simple way to extend the reach of the clamps is to double them up. To do this, interlock the tail portions of the clamps as shown in the top photo. Although this method works fine for light pressure, you may want to clamp the tail portions together with a C-clamp to keep them from slipping apart under heavier pressure.

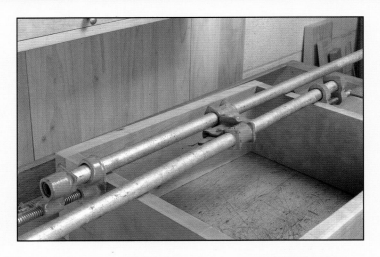

Couplers

Another way to lengthen your pipe clamps is to keep some pipe couplers on hand. Black pipe couplings like the one shown in the middle photo cost less than a buck and can be used to connect two of your pipe clamps together. I keep a couple of spare 3- and 4-foot lengths of black pipe around just for this purpose. I slide the end of the clamp off the pipe, add a coupler and the desired spare black pipe, slip the clamp end back on, and voilà—an instant pipe-stretcher.

Even pressure

This is one of my favorite tips for pipe clamps, which will really improve your ability to glue up flat panels. The heads of pipe clamps tend to tilt when tightened, resulting in an uneven pressure. To get around this, insert a dowel (or a rounded-over scrap piece) between the clamp heads and the workpiece (*bottom drawing*). The dowel both centers the clamping pressure on the workpiece edge and helps distribute it evenly.

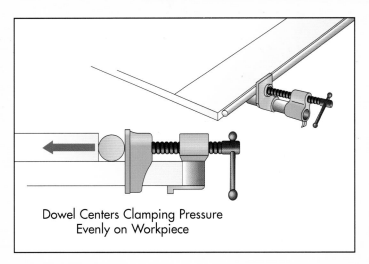

Dowel Centers Clamping Pressure
Evenly on Workpiece

Preventing stains

The raw metal pipe used with pipe clamps can stain the surface of your workpiece when the iron in the pipe comes in contact with glue. To prevent this from happening, I apply a layer of masking tape to the top of the pipe (*top photo*). Not only does this prevent stains, but it also makes it easy to remove dried glue from the clamps: Just peel off the tape, and the pipe is clean.

Plywood insert

Clamping up a case or carcass with pipe clamps can be a challenge, since the case often has a tendency to rack out of square under the pressure of the clamps. One way to prevent this is to cut a plywood insert to fit just inside the case and hold it square when clamps are applied (*middle drawing*). Screwing a pair of cleats to the insert will hold it in place while you apply clamps.

Spreader

You can turn a pipe clamp into a spreader by threading the ends of two pipe clamps together, as shown in the bottom photo. Spreaders are a great nondestructive way to push parts apart for repair, such as when re-gluing the rungs on a wobbly chair. The trick is to use slow, even pressure and make sure to pad the jaws of the clamp to prevent them from marring the workpiece surface.

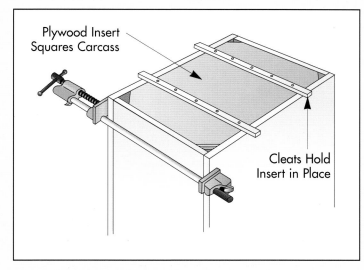

Plywood Insert Squares Carcass

Cleats Hold Insert in Place

BAR CLAMPS

Sliding bar clamps

Of all the clamps in my shop, sliding bar clamps are what I reach for most often (*top photo*). In fact, I keep them in a rack directly behind my bench so they're right at hand. These clamps feature a fixed jaw that's attached to a steel bar, and a sliding jaw with adjustable screw that can quickly open or close the jaws. Quality sliding bar clamps (Bessey's are my favorite: www.jamesmorton.com) come with plastic pads to cover the jaws and protect the work. They're available in jaw capacities from 4" to 38" and with varying reach (depth).

Aluminum bar clamps

I became quite attached to a set of aluminum bar clamps I used in a production shop several years ago (*middle drawing*). They are extremely lightweight and easy to work with. You might think they'd bend under pressure, and you'd be right—they do. So what good are they? Well, here again, if you need to exert heavy pressure to close up gaps, something is wrong. If you've done your work with care, these clamps will get the job done. Jorgensen (www.adjustableclamp.com) still sells these in various lengths, although you generally need to special-order them.

Steel I-beam clamps

Steel I-beam clamps are the bruisers of the clamping world. These heavy-duty clamps can exert wood-crushing force. They feature heavy castings and an I-shaped steel beam (*bottom drawing*), which keeps the beam from bowing under the considerable pressure these clamps produce. I-beam clamps are popular in professional shops because they don't bow with use over time, as pipe clamps will. If used judiciously, these are great clamps. In the hands of a "Popeye"-type clamper, they can do more damage than good.

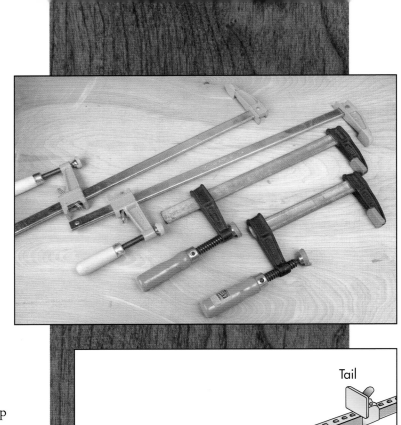

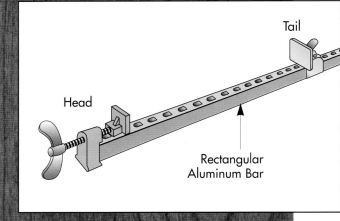

Tail

Head

Rectangular
Aluminum Bar

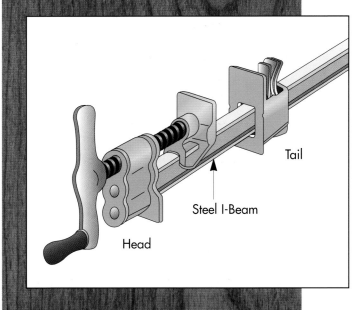

Tail

Steel I-Beam

Head

The first time I used a Bessey K-body clamp (www.jamesmorton.com), I was skeptical (*top photo*). According to the manufacturer, the jaws of the clamp were guaranteed to remain parallel as pressure was applied, unlike many other clamps where the jaws tilt under pressure. I was pleasantly surprised to find out they work great. They work so well that I continue to buy more as my budget allows. That's the only downside to these clamps: They're expensive (about $50 for a 4-foot clamp) but well worth it.

CLAMPING RULES

⬛ Rule #1: Always dry-clamp

One of the most reliable ways to prevent clamping problems is to dry-clamp your project before you reach for the glue bottle. Dry-clamping does a couple of things. First, it double-checks that all the parts fit well together. This might seem obvious, but I've seen a lot of woodworkers smear on glue and start assembly, only to find a tenon that doesn't fit in a mortise, or a rail or cleat that's too short. Dry-clamping prevents this annoying problem. It also is a good way to check for clamp placement—and just as important, to make sure you've got enough clamps on hand. Finally, it gets the clamps adjusted the proper distance to span the workpiece so that assembly will go quickly. And this is particularly important if you're working with yellow glue, since it has a relatively short open time (about 15 minutes).

⬛ Rule #2: Protect the workpiece

Since clamps can apply a lot of pressure, they're capable of marring your workpiece. Take the time to pad every clamp to protect the surface of the workpiece (*see page* 162). You should also protect the workpiece from excess glue. The best way is to apply the right amount in the first place so that it doesn't squeeze out onto the workpiece.

If you do encounter excess squeeze-out, wipe off the surplus with a clean, damp cloth.

⬛ Rule #3: Position the clamps for uniform pressure

Make sure your clamps are positioned parallel to the sides and edges of a workpiece (unless you're intentionally trying to rack the workpiece back into square; *see page* 163). Center the clamps on the workpiece and space them evenly. When gluing up panels, take care to distribute the clamping pressure evenly on the panel (*see page* 164).

⬛ Rule #4: Don't overclamp

Next to skipping the dry-clamping stage, overclamping is one of the main reasons glue-ups fail. The problem is that clamps are capable of exerting a lot of pressure, especially the steel I-beam type. And it's all too tempting to just crank down a little harder to tighten up the gap in that joint. Don't do it. You'll crush the wood, and in the long run, the wood will have its way and likely split. Here's another advantage of dry-clamping. If something doesn't fit right, take it apart and tweak the joint until it does. If everything fits properly, you shouldn't need to apply a lot of pressure. What you're looking for is an even bead of glue squeeze-out at the joints. Excess pressure creates a "starved" joint—all the glue is forced out, leaving nothing behind to create a bond.

THE WORKBENCH

My favorite clamp in my entire shop is my workbench. That's right, my workbench. The classic Ulmia bench I picked up almost 25 years ago is still my favorite clamping tool (*top photo*). It features a pair of vises (one front, one tail) and a built-in tool tray. Naturally, the vises provide a lot of clamping capacity, but what really makes this bench my favorite are the bench dogs and dog holes. Bench dogs are wood or metal bars that fit into holes along the length of the bench and into holes in the tail vise.

The beauty of this arrangement is that you can clamp a workpiece almost as long as the bench to the surface without any additional clamps. Just insert one bench dog in the tail vise, position the workpiece, and then open or close the vise until a hole is exposed at the end of the workpiece. Slip in a dog and tighten the vise. An added benefit of this system is that the dogs can be adjusted up or down to keep them below the surface of the workpiece. This means you can work on the entire surface at once, something that's essential when planing, scraping, or sanding a surface.

When shopping for a bench, look for stout legs, a thick top, and two vises, including a tail vise with bench dog holes (*bottom drawing*). Note that if you find a bench you like and it doesn't have bench dogs, you can add these after the fact (*see the sidebar on page* 170). Also, if you find you can't afford the bench you want, consider making one. Woodsmith sells an excellent set of plans for a classic European-style workbench (www.augusthome.com).

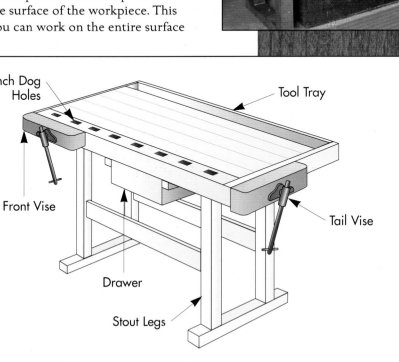

Bench Dog Holes

Tool Tray

Front Vise

Tail Vise

Drawer

Stout Legs

BENCH VISES

A workbench without a solid vise is like a power sander without electricity. You could still sand with it by rubbing it on the workpiece, but why not use it to its full potential? To really get the most out of a sturdy workbench, you'll need to install at least one (preferably two) quality woodworking vises. Record vises (*top photo*) have long been a favorite of woodworkers (www.recordtools.com). In particular, their model $52^{1}/_{2}$ED, with its 9" jaws and 13" opening, is well regarded as one of the better all-purpose woodworking vises. Most of Record's vises incorporate their patented "Quick-release" feature that lets you open and close the jaws quickly without having to turn the screw (*inset*).

A quality bench vise should have beefy castings and an adjustable front dog that can be used to clamp workpieces to the top of the bench. The fixed jaw of the vise is generally "let in" or mortised into the front edge of the bench; the adjustable jaw moves in and out as the main screw is rotated by the handle (*bottom drawing*). Both jaws of the vise should be lined with wood to prevent damage to the workpiece.

Photos courtesy of American Tool Companies, Inc., copyright 2001

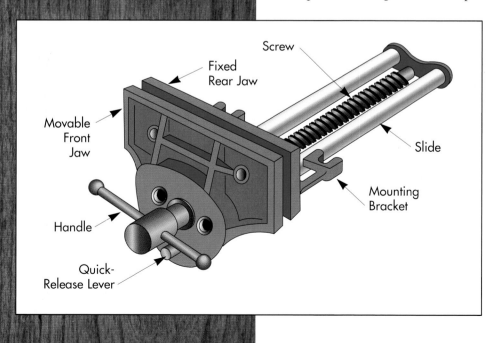

Screw

Fixed Rear Jaw

Movable Front Jaw

Slide

Handle

Mounting Bracket

Quick-Release Lever

Mounting a bench vise can be simple or complicated. It's simple if you just bolt it to the front edge of the bench and screw it to the underside. The problem with this is that a workpiece that's clamped in the vise will always protrude from the front edge of the bench. This isn't a big deal for a short workpiece, but if the workpiece is long, it's difficult to clamp the unsupported end to the edge of the bench.

This problem goes away when you mount the vise so the fixed jaw ends up flush with the workbench edge (actually, so the wood liner attached to the fixed jaw is flush with the front edge). To mount a vise this way, you'll need to cut a notch in the front edge of the bench to accept the vise and liner (*top drawing*). In many cases, it'll also be necessary to insert a filler piece or shim between the mounting plate and the underside of the bench; consult your vise mounting instructions for details. NOTE: Even high-quality vises can "rack" or twist out of square if you clamp a short piece in the vise. To prevent this, just insert a scrap of similar thickness at the opposite end of the vise to evenly distribute the pressure (*middle drawing*).

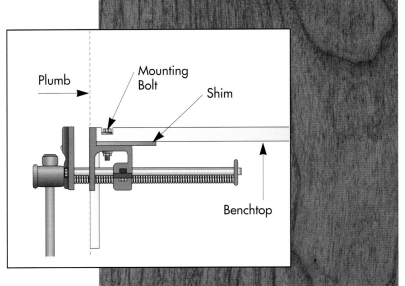

Plumb

Mounting Bolt

Shim

Benchtop

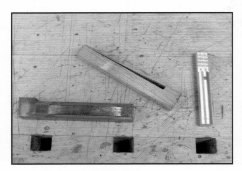

Workpiece

Scrap Block

BENCH DOGS

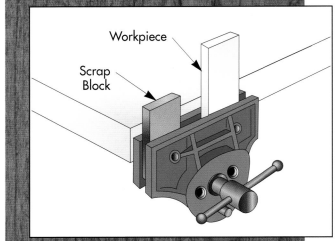

Although they have a funny name, bench dogs are an important part of a functioning workbench (*photo at right*). They can be square, rectangular, or round and fit into correspondingly shaped holes in the top. If you buy a bench with rectangular dogs (like my Ulmia), I recommend that you make wooden versions. All it takes is one slip of a sharp chisel into a metal dog to understand why. Also, if your bench doesn't have dogs, you can buy round ones and simply drill a series of holes in the benchtop.

SPECIALTY VISES

Carver's vise

A carver's vise (*top vise in drawing at left*) is a portable unit that can be clamped to any sturdy edge. The workpiece is attached to the round mounting plate, which can then be adjusted for height, angle, and rotation. This makes it easy for the carver to do 360-degree work without having to move around. Instead, the workpiece is adjusted into the optimal position for carving.

Patternmaker's vise

A patternmaker's vise (*middle vise in drawing at left*) is a special type of woodworker's vise that can be rotated or be flipped horizontal or vertical and that accepts tapered work. Sounds great; what's the catch? This vise will cost easily 3 to 4 times what a conventional bench vise would. I have a friend who has one of these, and although he likes it just fine, he's found that he rarely uses the special features. He has also noted that it doesn't hold up well under heavy use, such as when he's chopping mortises.

Bench holdfast

A bench holdfast (or hold-down) is used to press a workpiece firmly against the top of the workbench so that it can be worked on (*bottom vise in drawing at left*). The holdfast consists of a shaft with a pivoting arm and swivel shoe. The shaft fits into a metal collar let into the bench-top. Tightening a screw on the end of the pivoting arm forces the swivel shoe into the workpiece. These are commonly used by carvers to hold down work in progress.

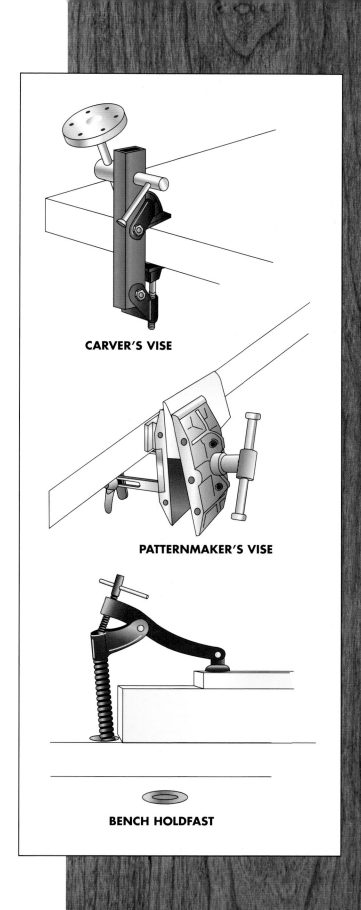

CARVER'S VISE

PATTERNMAKER'S VISE

BENCH HOLDFAST

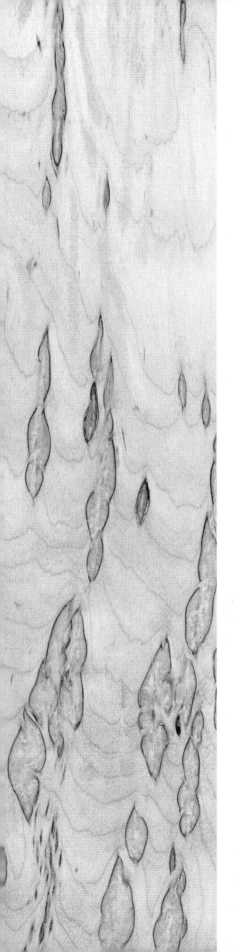

"The expectations of life depend on diligence: The mechanic that would perfect his work must first sharpen his tools."

CONFUCIUS (551 BC – 479 BC)

SHARPENING TOOLS

I would dare amend Confucius' words this way: To perfect your work *and keep yourself from harm*, first sharpen your tools. I have a hand scar as a souvenir of forcing a dull tool. If it'd been sharp, the ¼" chisel would have sliced cleanly through wood. But it wasn't; instead it cleanly pierced my right palm. That was the day I learned that there is nothing more dangerous in the shop than a dull tool. Some days later, the day I learned how to put a razor-sharp edge on a chisel, was the day I became a better woodworker.

You know how frustrating it is to fight with a dull tool. Like many woodworkers, I once assumed that a brand-new tool was ready to go. But I learned otherwise: Most brand-new tools are not sharp. Although they're ground to the correct angle, they're not honed. Until you hone it, it's darn near useless. So you can avoid frustration, botched jobs, and personal injury by knowing more about your sharpening options. Oilstones, waterstones, honing guides, grinding wheels, burnishers—they all have a role to play, if you know when and how to use them.

Row 1 (top) left to right: flexible-neck oil can; sharpening stones; bench-mounted hand-crank grinder for sharpening smaller objects. Row 2: boxed oilstone, Norton "Quickcut" boxed carborundum sharpening stone; black oilstone. Row 3: Record edge-tool honer for sharpening chisels, plane blades, etc.; Disston hand-saw jointer; Otis A. Smith, Rockfall, Connecticut, adjustable saw set.

Sharpening Terminology

For an edge to be truly sharp, the two surfaces that meet to form the bevel angle must be flat and honed the same amount (*top photo*). This somewhat obvious fact is one of the most commonly overlooked factors involved in sharpening tools. I've seen plenty of woodworkers spend considerable time and effort honing a bevel to a mirror finish, only to ignore the back. Both must be honed to the same degree of finish for the surfaces to meet cleanly at the edge (*middle drawing*).

Although there are a lot of different-edged tools in the workshop, you'll likely spend most of your time sharpening plane blades and chisels. There are four common ways to handle the grinding and honing of these edges: a flat grind, a flat grind with a microbevel, a hollow grind, and a hollow grind with a microbevel (*bottom drawing*). Which you use is really a matter of preference.

Personally, I prefer to hollow-grind the edges of my cutting tools (the hollow results from creating the bevel on a grinding wheel). The big advantage to this is that there's a lot less material to remove when you hone the bevel. Since the bevel is concave, only the toe and heel will rest on the stone, and only these surfaces

will be honed. With a flat grind, the entire bevel rests on the stone unless you choose to use a microbevel. The advantage to this is the same as for a hollow grind—less material to be removed means faster honing.

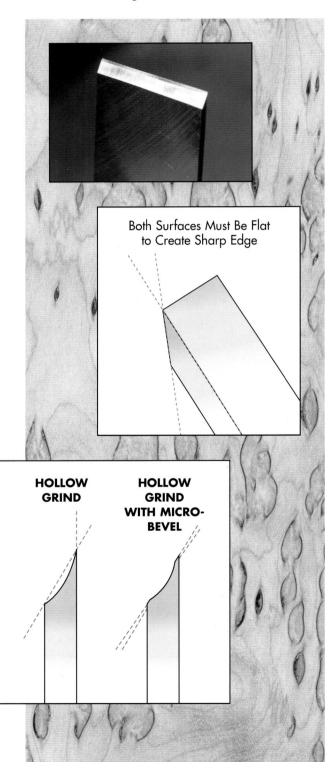

Both Surfaces Must Be Flat to Create Sharp Edge

FLAT   FLAT GRIND WITH MICROBEVEL   HOLLOW GRIND   HOLLOW GRIND WITH MICRO-BEVEL

Natural Oilstones

When I first delved into sharpening some 25 years ago, man-made stones (*see page* 176) were of questionable quality, and the only reasonable choice was to use natural stones. I still have the original oilstones I bought back then and am glad I do. It's increasingly hard to find quality oilstones (especially in the larger bench stone sizes), as the deposits have already been systematically mined. The most famous of these are the novaculite deposits in Arkansas. Novaculite is a natural abrasive that holds up extremely well over time.

Varying grits

Arkansas stones are available in four grits. From coarse to fine, they are Washita (*top photo*), soft Arkansas (*middle photo*), hard Arkansas (*bottom photo*), and black hard Arkansas (*bottom inset*). A light machine oil or honing oil is the lubricant of choice with these stones and, if used in progression, can create a razor-sharp edge on your tools.

Although I have switched primarily to using waterstones (*see page* 177), I still often use my oilstones because they require less setup time and definitely create much less mess than waterstones. This makes them particularly handy when I just need to touch up an edge. I pull out the desired stone, add a dollop of oil, and sharpen away. A quick wipe of a clean cloth and the tool is ready for use, and the oilstone can go back on the shelf. Contrast this to the water mess created when sharpening with waterstones, and it's easy to see why I still use these. If your budget allows for both oilstones and waterstones, terrific. If I had to choose one, I'd go with the faster-cutting waterstones.

MAN-MADE STONES

A number of abrasives manufacturers (like Norton and 3M) make artificial oilstones, and produce them in many shapes and sizes (*top photo*). Particularly useful are the larger, wider bench stones that are necessary for sharpening plane blades. Another convenient feature of man-made stones is that they are often made with two grits and are sandwiched together in a single stone (*middle drawing*).

I've tried a number of different man-made stones and for the most part have not found one that I felt was as rugged as a natural stone. True, many of these stones are more aggressive, but this also means they wear more quickly—and truing a natural or artificial oilstone is more work then truing up a waterstone. Before I'd invest in a set of man-made oilstones, I'd buy a set of man-made waterstones.

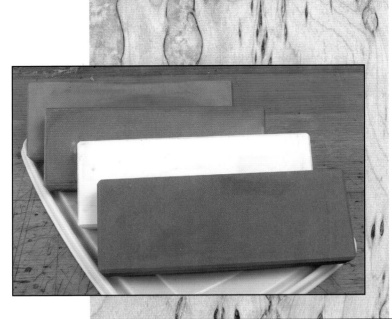

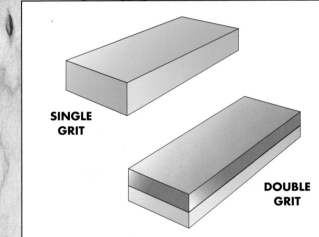

SINGLE GRIT

DOUBLE GRIT

TRUING A STONE

For any stone to do its job, it must be flat. All stones tend to wear with use and tend to "dish out" in the middle, as this area sees the most use. The best way I've found to true up an oilstone (either man-made or natural) is to rub it on a coarse diamond stone; another option is to use a lapping plate with silicon-carbide particles (*see page* 181). Since waterstones

are softer than oilstones, they wear more quickly but are easier to true up. The simplest way to do this is to true up a fine stone with a coarser one by rubbing them gently together. For any of this to work, your coarsest stone must be flat. I've found that a piece of drywall screen on a flat surface works well for this (*photo above left*). Make sure that you thoroughly flush each stone after truing to remove all traces of the coarser grit.

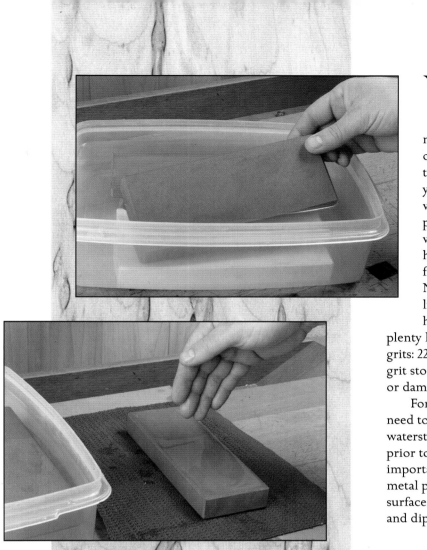

WATERSTONES

I can't imagine woodworking without my waterstones. To me, they're far superior to other stones because they cut so fast to quickly produce a keen edge. Although you can still purchase natural Japanese waterstones, their high cost is usually prohibitive. In recent years, man-made waterstones that are much cheaper have hit the market. The stones I've been using for a while now are manufactured by Norton (www.nortonabrasives.com). I like these because they're wide enough to handle my widest plane blade and they're plenty long (8"×3"×1"). They're available in four grits: 220, 1000, 4000, and 8000. I use the 220-grit stone only for shaping or repairing a nicked or damaged blade.

For waterstones to work effectively, they need to be thoroughly wet. You should soak a waterstone in clean water for at least 10 minutes prior to use (*top photo*). As you use the stone, it's important to keep the surface wet to prevent metal particles from becoming lodged in the surface (*middle photo*). I keep water right at hand and dip my hand in periodically to drip additional water on the stone.

Since I'm continually sharpening my tools, I prefer to store my stones in water. This way they're always ready to use. A plastic storage box with a tight-fitting lid works well for this. ShopTip: To eliminate the possibility of mold or mildew growing in the plastic box, add a capful of household bleach to the box every time you change the water (*bottom photo*). Caution: Be careful not to leave your stored stones in an unheated garage. If the water freezes, odds are the stones will crack and you'll end up with some really expensive slipstones.

GRINDING WHEELS

When a tool edge gets damaged or needs to be reshaped, an electric or hand-powered grinder is the tool for the job. The problem many woodworkers have with power grinding is twofold. First, most grinders turn at 3450 rpm—this is just too fast. Even with the right wheel, this speed can quickly remove the temper from a tool, rendering it useless. Recently, slower-rpm grinders (1800 rpm) have become available and are well worth the extra money. The second problem is that the wheels that come standard on most grinders are like the blades that come on power saws—they're useless. These wheels are usually very coarse and very hard. They'll burn an edge in seconds. Take them off, throw them away, and replace them with wheels intended for use in sharpening tools.

What you're looking for is basically the Japanese waterstone equivalent in a wheel: The wheel needs to be soft and fine and have a fairly open coat. Like a waterstone, this will cut aggressively but wear quickly. I've used a Norton 80-grit aluminum-oxide wheel successfully for years. It removes a lot of metal in a hurry while minimizing the risk of burning—a great all-purpose sharpening wheel (*white wheel in the top photo*).

WHEEL DRESSERS

With use, the surface of any grinding wheel will clog up with metal particles. When this happens, the wheel loses its cutting ability and needs to be "dressed": that is, scraped clean to reveal a fresh grinding surface. There are a number of wheel dressers on the market just for this job. Two of the more common are the abrasive stick (*photo at far right*) and the star-wheel dresser (*photo at near right*). I use an abrasive stick more often than my star-wheel dresser, as it leaves a smoother surface. To true up an out-of-round wheel, I have a diamond dresser that resembles a ballpoint pen except it's tipped with a 1/4-carat industrial diamond. These are available from most woodworking catalogs and cost less than $20.

HONING GUIDES

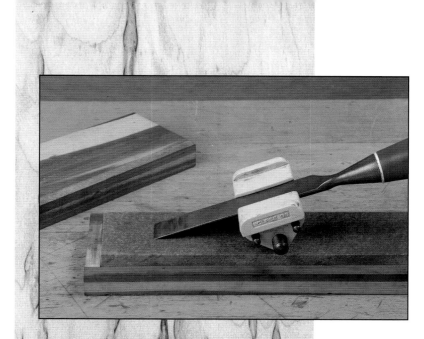

A honing guide is designed to rigidly hold a tool at a constant angle for honing. Although I have met a few accomplished cabinetmakers who hone without a guide, most woodworkers will benefit from the added reinforcement one offers. There are numerous honing guides available through mail-order catalogs and at your local hardware store or home center. There are two basic types of guides: the type that grips the tool and rolls on the stone (*top photo*) and the larger type where the guide roller rests on the adjacent surface (*middle photo*).

I'm quite partial to the smaller type of honing guide that rolls on the stone along with the tool. The one I've used for years is an Eclipse No. 35 honing guide, which clamps the blade or chisel between two jaws. The beauty of this guide is that it automatically centers the tool. Since it runs on the stone, there's no chance of error caused by an uneven surface—as is possible with the other type.

Setting the guide

There are a number of ways to set a honing guide. If the blade or chisel has been ground to the desired bevel, you can use this to position the guide. Slide the tool up or down in the guide until both the toe and heel of the bevel rest flat on the stone (*bottom drawing*), and begin honing. Alternatively, angle-setting guides are available for the Eclipse jig that will accurately position the tool at the desired angle (www.leevalley.com).

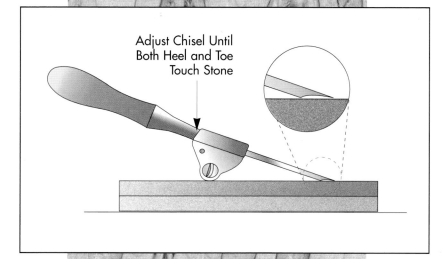

Adjust Chisel Until Both Heel and Toe Touch Stone

STROPS

Certain types of leather contain a natural abrasive that makes them ideal for touching up an edge. I'm sure you've seen a strop in action at a barbershop, where they've traditionally been used to create a super-fine edge on a straight razor. These long flexible strops (*top photo*) work well for this but are generally too flexible for most woodworking tools (with the exception of some knives). A better alternative is a paddle-type strop, where a piece of leather is fastened to a wood paddle or block (*middle photo*). This less-flexible strop works better for both straight-edged and curved tools.

Strops are particularly popular with carvers, as they permit quickly restoring a keen edge without the mess of either oil or water. You can vary the aggressiveness of the strop by "charging" the surface with different grits of rouge. Simply rub the rouge on the surface in the same direction as you'd use for honing—usually a trailing stroke; that is, the body of the tool is always moved so the bevel "trails" it. In stropping the other way, with the edge leading the tool, it will dig in and possibly cut the leather.

SLIPSTONES

Slipstones are another favorite of carvers. These are small, odd-shaped stones that are designed to "slip" into the rounded and V-shaped edges of carving tools (*photo at right*). They are available in a variety of shapes and sizes, different materials (both natural and man-made), and numerous grits. For the most part, I use these primarily to remove a burr on the inside edge of a carving tool that I've created with a regular stone.

LAPPING PLATES AND DIAMOND STONES

Lapping plates

A lapping plate is any reference surface that can be used to create a flat surface on a tool. I use lapping plates regularly to flatten the soles of planes (*top photo*) and to flatten sharpening stones. The plate I use is a piece of $1/4$"-thick glass that is actually a replacement louver for a Jalousie window. These louvers have the edges conveniently rounded-over. Since there is still a bit of flex in one of these, it's important to place it on a known-flat surface. The abrasive action is supplied by sheets of silicon-carbide paper mounted to the glass with spray adhesive.

Photo courtesy of DMT (Diamond Machining Technologies), Inc., copyright 2001

Diamond stones

Although they're expensive, diamond stones and hones are well worth the money (*middle photo*). Diamond stones are made by bonding uniform-sized diamond particles to a metal plate and attaching this to a polycarbonate base. Since diamonds are the hardest material known, they wear very slowly and the stone will stay "sharp" for a very long time. Diamond stones and hones are available in many shapes and sizes and in four grits: extra-coarse (220 mesh), coarse (325 mesh), fine (600 mesh), and extra-fine (1200 mesh). I use stones made by DMT (www.dmtsharp. com) and have yet to wear one out.

Basic use

You can use a diamond stone just like you would a waterstone (water is the recommended lubricant), but you'll notice a few differences (*bottom photo*). First, unlike waterstones, diamond stones won't dish out: They stay flat. And second, they'll actually cut faster in most situations because the diamonds stay sharp so long—you'll end up taking fewer strokes (what a pity, eh?).

SHARPENING EDGE TOOLS

The sharpening method described here has served me well for years. I use waterstones and start with a medium grit and work my way up to my finest stone, which leaves a mirror finish. I prefer to both flatten the back and then hone the edge with one grit before advancing to the next.

Flatten the back

The first step in sharpening an edged tool is to flatten the back. Although only the ¼" or so nearest the end needs to be flat, I've seen woodworkers spend hours flattening the entire back to a mirror finish. This might look spiffy, but it doesn't make the blade any sharper. Select the appropriate stone (*see pages 175–177*) and lubricant, and apply firm downward pressure to the blade as you move it back and forth over the full length of the stone (*top photo*). Stop when you can feel a burr on the bevel side.

Set the guide

Once you've created a burr, the next step is to remove it by honing the bevel. Although you can do this free-hand, I recommend some type of honing guide (*see page 179*) to hold the blade at a fixed angle. How you set the guide will depend on the guide and the tool you're honing. In most cases, after you insert the tool in the guide, you'll slide it back and forth until the sharpening angle is reached, then tighten the guide (*middle photo*).

Hone the bevel

Honing the bevel is the trickiest part to sharpening—especially if you're working on a narrow tool like a chisel. There's a natural tendency to rock the tool as you slide it back and forth over the stone. The best way I've found to avoid this is to press down on both corners of

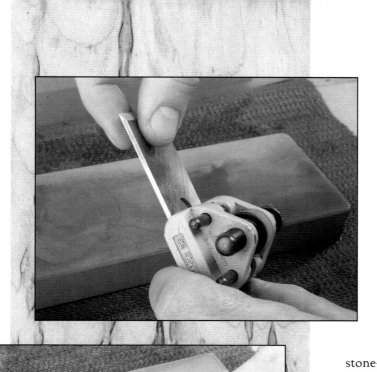

the blade and lock my elbows in tight against my body (*bottom photo on opposite page*). Take a few strokes and look at the bevel. If it's lopsided, compensate by pressing more on one side.

Remove the burr

After you've honed the edge, check to see whether you've created a burr by sliding your finger gently up the back of the blade (*top photo*). Then flip the blade over and take a few strokes to remove the burr. The whole idea behind sharpening is to create increasingly finer burrs on the blade's edge. It's important to remove the burr before progressing to the next stone, as the burr can score the surface of the stone—especially the softer waterstones.

Change grits

Depending on which stone you started with, you can move up to the next-finest grit. If, for example, the tool was relatively sharp and just needed a touchup, you may have begun with your finest stone. If not, switch stones and repeat the process of flattening the back, honing the bevel and removing the burr until the edge is razor-sharp (*middle photo*). When is it sharp? I don't recommend the old "shaving the arm hair" trick. If the tool can cleanly shave end grain, it's sharp enough for me.

Add a microbevel

You may or may not want to create a microbevel on the edge once the blade is sharp (*bottom photo*). Some honing guides have a built-in cam that can be rotated to raise the blade (typically around 1 to 2 degrees) to hone the bevel. Sometimes when I want to touch up a blade, it's faster to create a microbevel than it is to sharpen the entire bevel, since I'm removing a whole lot less metal.

SHARPENING SAWS

I've always found sharpening a saw very rewarding. It's a fairly straightforward job that takes less than half an hour and produces immediate results.

Jointing the teeth

The first step in sharpening a handsaw is to create an even playing field; that is, filing all the teeth to the same level so that no single tooth does more work than the others (*top drawing*). When this happens, the protruding tooth quickly dulls from doing most of the work and ends up tearing wood fibers instead of cleanly slicing through them. To prevent this, the saw is "jointed" by running a smooth mill file over the tops of the teeth. The simplest way to hold the file perpendicular to the saw is to cut a kerf in a block of wood along its length to accept the file. Then insert the file in the kerf and set the file on the teeth. Press the scrap into the side of the saw and file until you can see a bright spot on the tip of each and every tooth.

Setting the teeth

The next step is to "set" the teeth by alternately bending them away from the saw at a specific angle. This is done with a special tool called a saw set, which can be picked up at almost any auction for a couple of bucks. Saw sets are adjustable so that you can vary the amount of set to match the saw. The general rule of thumb is that the set should equal one-half the thickness of the tooth (*middle drawing*). A saw set should be adjusted so that it sets only the top one-half of the tooth; and you should never reverse the set of a tooth, as it will weaken it substantially.

Adding blocks as guides

For me, the biggest challenge to sharpening a saw is keeping track of which teeth have been sharpened and which teeth haven't. I solved this dilemma by sliding scraps of thin wood

between the saw blade and jaws of my shop-made saw vise (*see the sidebar on the opposite page*). I raise the scraps up far enough so that as I sharpen each tooth, it leaves a telltale mark on the guide (*bottom photo*). This makes it child's play to track sharpening progress and allows me to concentrate instead on sharpening.

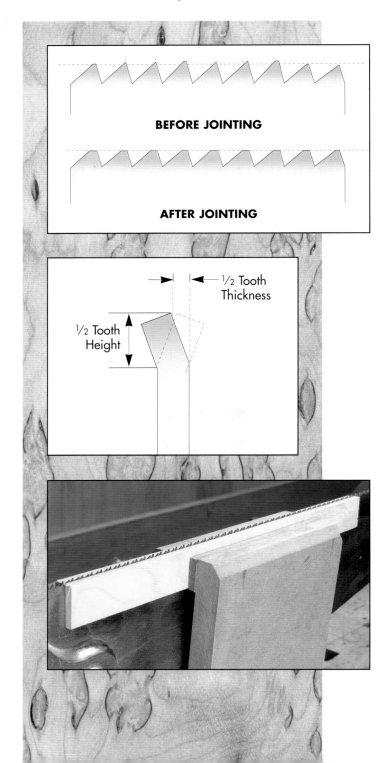

BEFORE JOINTING

AFTER JOINTING

½ Tooth Height

½ Tooth Thickness

Sharpening one side

I think sharpening is the easy part. In most cases, all you want to do is maintain the original sharpening angles. To do this, gently place a slim taper file in one of the gullets of the saw. You'll notice that it will almost immediately align itself with the existing angle. All you have to do then is hold it at this angle and take a few strokes (*top photo*). The key thing here then is to maintain this angle while taking the identical number of strokes for each tooth. On crosscut saws, you'll need to sharpen every other tooth at this angle, then flip the saw and do the other side (*see below*). This work goes surprisingly quick because it's easy to drift into a rhythm—three strokes, skip a tooth, three strokes, etc.

Sharpening the other side

If you're sharpening a rip saw, all the teeth are filed at the same angle—just hold the saw perpendicular to the saw blade, and progress down the blade, sharpening every tooth in turn. Crosscut saws, with their opposing angled teeth, require that you flip the saw to sharpen the teeth you skipped earlier. The technique here is the same, and if you use the scrap blocks again, you'll create a crisscross pattern that will track your sharpening progress (*middle photo*).

SHOP-MADE SAW VISE

Although you could clamp a saw in a bench vise for sharpening, you'll find that it's a lot easier with a saw vise. A saw vise grips a wide portion of the blade and raises the blade up to a comfortable working height. You can occasionally find a saw vise at an auction, or you can make your own out of a couple scraps and some inexpensive hardware (*drawing at right*). The saw vise is just a couple pieces of hardwood that are lined at the top and bottom with strips of hardboard to create jaws. A carriage bolt and a wing nut or threaded knob supply the clamping pressure.

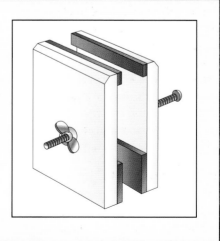

SHARPENING SCRAPERS

The magic behind a scraper is the burr. This burr is a tiny metal edge that's rolled or "burnished" with a special tool called a burnisher. As a general rule of thumb, the burr is rolled at an angle between 80 and 85 degrees on a flat-edged scraper (*top drawing*). Bevel-edged scrapers, such as those used in cabinet scrapers and scraper planes, are rolled at 35 to 40 degrees. Over the years, I've seen a lot of woodworkers struggle with sharpening a scraper. If you follow the simple method shown here, the same that I've used to teach numerous classes, I'm confident you'll be creating whisper-thin shavings in no time.

Filing the scraper flat

The first step in sharpening a scraper is to file the edges perfectly flat. Just clamp the scraper in your bench vise (with wood liners, of course) and take a few strokes across the top edge with a smooth mill file (*middle photo*).

Honing the edge

After the edges of the scraper are flat, the next thing to do is hone them smooth. NOTE: I have successfully skipped this step on occasion; but if you want a uniform burr, especially if you're looking for super-fine shavings, it's well worth the effort to hone the edge. Since holding a scraper on edge vertically so it's perfectly perpendicular is virtually impossible, I use a trick I learned from master chairmaker Brian Boggs. Brian sandwiches the scraper between two wood blocks to hold the scraper in perfect position and then rubs this "sandwich" on the stone (*bottom photo*). Note that it's important to skew the sandwich as shown in the bottom photo to prevent the thin edge of the scraper from scoring a groove in your stone.

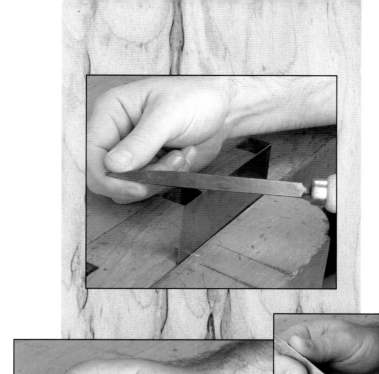

Burnishing at 90 degrees

Once you've honed the edges of the scraper smooth, it's time to get out the burnisher (*see the sidebar below*). I begin burnishing with the burnisher held perpendicular to the face of the scraper. I take several strokes with moderate downward pressure along the entire edge of the scraper (*top photo*). This will compress the metal and actually create a small burr, which you should be able to feel by running your thumb up from under the edge. In some cases, this may be all the burr you need. If you're planning on removing a lot of material, you'll want a larger burr and you'll need to burnish the edge at an angle.

Burnishing at an angle

Hold the burnisher at 80 to 85 degrees for a flat-edged scraper (*middle photo*) and around 40 degrees for an angle-edged scraper (*inset*). Apply light pressure and take a few strokes. Check the burr and repeat if it's not large enough. You might be surprised how little pressure is typically needed to create a burr. I've seen guys pressing down so hard they were flexing the scraper. This shouldn't be necessary. If it is, it's likely that your burnisher isn't hard enough to roll the burr (*see below*).

BURNISHERS

A burnisher must have two features to work properly: The steel must be harder than the scraper (Rc 60 at a minimum), and it must be super-smooth to prevent damage to the delicate burr. You can get a burnisher for a couple bucks from most woodworking catalogs (*photo at near right*). In a pinch, I've used the shank of a large drill bit—just be sure to protect your hands with gloves (*photo at far right*). Also, take the time to smooth the surface of the burnisher with a fine sharpening stone or by buffing it with a felt wheel and some jeweler's rouge.

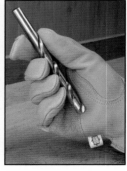

APPENDIX:
Restoring Old Hand Tools

I love to bring an old hand tool back to life. I often scrounge auctions and yard sales, looking for likely candidates. As long as the castings are sound and the tool is in reasonable condition (and dirt cheap), I'll adopt it and bring it home. Keep in mind that I'm interested in using the tool, so I'll often do more to it than a collector would. Most tool collectors are interested in preserving the tool's patina, and that's fine. But the once-over I give a tool (described here) would put most collectors in shock. If you're interested in collecting tools and want to learn more about what you should or shouldn't do to an antique, visit the Mid-West Tool Collectors Association website at www.mwtca.org. They're a great organization.

Disassemble and clean

To start work on an old tool, I begin by taking it completely apart (*top photo*). This lets me check the condition of all the parts and makes them easier to clean. I'll clean most parts with a mild detergent solution, and if pitch and resin have built up, I'll scrub this away with a cloth or nonwoven abrasive pad dipped in acetone, mineral spirits, or lacquer thinner (*middle photo*).

Remove rust

Next, I'll tackle any rusty areas (*bottom photo*). Depending on whether it's surface rust or heavily pitted, this can require anything from scrubbing the part with a Wonderbar (a great product) to using a wire brush, or even the magic of electrolysis (*see the sidebar on the opposite page*).

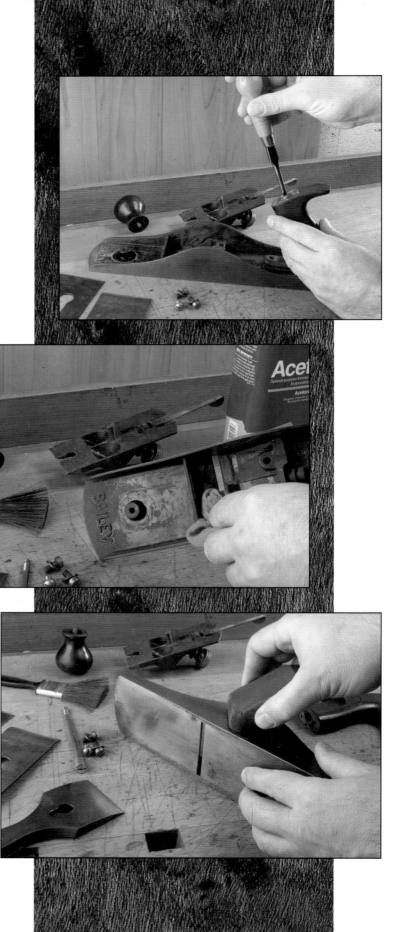

Sharpen parts if necessary

If the tool employs a part with a cutting edge, I'll sharpen the edge using my standard sharpening technique (*top photo*). For more on sharpening, see pages 182–183.

Reassemble

When all the parts are clean, free from rust, and sharp (if applicable), I'll put the tool back together (*middle photo*). As I do this, I'll add a drop or two of light machine oil to linkages and will usually apply a coat of paste wax to cast-iron surfaces to help prevent future rust. If the tool has wood parts (like the plane shown here), I'll usually apply a light coat of tung oil to them to help keep out dirt and grime. Then on to the best part—using the tool—what better way to spend an afternoon in the shop!

REMOVING RUST WITH ELECTROLYSIS

Here's a slick way to remove rust from your tools using, of all things, electrolysis. Electrolysis passes a small electrical current from a battery charger through a rusty tool that's submerged in an electrolyte solution. An exchange of ions takes place, and the rust flakes away. Here's how to do it. First, mix up an electrolyte solution (1 tablespoon of baking powder per gallon of water) in a nonconductive, plastic container. Then, remove any nonmetallic parts from the tool. Now clamp the positive (red) lead of a 2-amp battery charger to an anode—an anode is just any large, flat piece of steel (like a kitchen pan lid). And connect the negative (black) lead to the rusty tool.

Slip the rusty tool and anode in the solution so they're a few inches apart. Make sure the tool is completely submerged and the red clip that's attached to the anode is above the solution to prevent it from corroding. Turn on the battery charger, and check that it's not drawing more current than it's rated for (this is where a built-in ammeter is indispensable). If it is drawing too much, or not enough, current, move the tool father away or closer to the anode. (SAFETY NOTE: make all of the adjustments with the charger unplugged!) You can tell it's working when you start to see bubbles forming on the surface of the tool. The average tool will de-rust in about two hours. Turn off the charger, put on rubber gloves to remove the tool, and unfasten the clips. You'll find a lot of black crud on the tool. The quickest way to remove any crud is with an abrasive pad. Just scrub the surface with a pad dipped in warm, soapy water. If the rust is gone, you're done. If not, repeat the process until it is.

INDEX

METRIC EQUIVALENCY CHART

Inches to millimeters and centimeters

inches	mm	cm	inches	cm	inches	cm
1/8	3	0.3	9	22.9	30	76.2
1/4	6	0.6	10	25.4	31	78.7
3/8	10	1.0	11	27.9	32	81.3
1/2	13	1.3	12	30.5	33	83.8
5/8	16	1.6	13	33.0	34	86.4
3/4	19	1.9	14	35.6	35	88.9
7/8	22	2.2	15	38.1	36	91.4
1	25	2.5	16	40.6	37	94.0
1 1/4	32	3.2	17	43.2	38	96.5
1 1/2	38	3.8	18	45.7	39	99.1
1 3/4	44	4.4	19	48.3	40	101.6
2	51	5.1	20	50.8	41	104.1
2 1/2	64	6.4	21	53.3	42	106.7
3	76	7.6	22	55.9	43	109.2
3 1/2	89	8.9	23	58.4	44	111.8
4	102	10.2	24	61.0	45	114.3
4 1/2	114	11.4	25	63.5	46	116.8
5	127	12.7	26	66.0	47	119.4
6	152	15.2	27	68.6	48	121.9
7	178	17.8	28	71.1	49	124.5
8	203	20.3	29	73.7	50	127.0

mm = millimeters   cm = centimeters